the COMMON GOOD

the COMMON GOOD

RISING OF A NEW DAWN

How Living a More Conscious Life
Can Heal a Nation
One Heart, One Mind, One Thought at a Time

JUANITA S. FARROW

New York

the COMMON GOOD
RISING OF A NEW DAWN
How Living a More Conscious Life Can Heal a Nation
One Heart, One Mind, One Thought at a Time

© 2016 Juanita S. Farrow.

Published in New York, New York, by Morgan James Publishing. Morgan James and The Entrepreneurial Publisher are trademarks of Morgan James, LLC.
www.MorganJamesPublishing.com

The Morgan James Speakers Group can bring authors to your live event. For more information or to book an event visit The Morgan James Speakers Group at www.TheMorganJamesSpeakersGroup.com.

Unless otherwise noted, all Scripture referenced comes from THE HOLY BIBLE, NEW INTERNATIONAL VERSION®, NIV® Copyright© 1973, 1978, 1984, 2011 by Biblica, Inc.® Used by permission. All rights reserved.

A **free** eBook edition is available with the purchase of this print book.

CLEARLY PRINT YOUR NAME ABOVE IN UPPER CASE
Instructions to claim your free eBook edition:
1. Download the BitLit app for Android or iOS
2. Write your name in **UPPER CASE** on the line
3. Use the BitLit app to submit a photo
4. Download your eBook to any device

ISBN 9781630476182 paperback
ISBN 9781630476199 eBook
Library of Congress Control Number:
2015905229

Cover Design by:
Rachel Lopez
www.r2cdesign.com

Interior Design by:
Bonnie Bushman
The Whole Caboodle Graphic Design

In an effort to support local communities and raise awareness and funds, Morgan James Publishing donates a percentage of all book sales for the life of each book to Habitat for Humanity Peninsula and Greater Williamsburg.

Get involved today, visit
www.MorganJamesBuilds.com

Habitat for Humanity®
Peninsula and
Greater Williamsburg
Building Partner

Contents

Preface

Business, politics, and religion. Separation of church and state. Separate, yet connected by the common good. A recovering economy, a toxic political environment, a religious community with declining church membership—not to mention the perpetual acts of terrorism and unrest around the world. It sounds like a perfect storm. One person thinks the world is doomed, yet another looks for the silver lining believing one day we will awaken to a new dawn.

I remember hearing my parents say, when I was just a kid, "Trouble don't last always." In the middle of the storm, the visibility is impaired. It's difficult to see beyond your immediate surroundings. But our nation is on the verge of a breakthrough; we are on the verge of a *new dawn* and may not even realize it. Many believe that the country is in need of a unifying, grassroots movement to heal the brokenness so evident in our society. But such a movement would require a lot of "heart."

Imagine if our business, political, and religious communities were all working for the "common good" of the people. Imagine if the words from the Pledge of Allegiance—which we so eloquently recite in sports arenas as we stand shoulder to shoulder to cheer on our favorite team—imagine if those words, "One Nation under God," became a guiding principle. What if we really believed we are ONE Nation under God, uniting for ONE people, ONE purpose? Imagine if we were not separated by religion or denominations, nor torn by growing income and wealth disparities. Imagine if we had a government that actually worked for the people—not just for the good of the special interest groups. Like Dorothy in *The Wizard of Oz*, we might learn that we never needed the Wizard to find our way back home. We had the power all along; we just needed to believe it.

The good news is we have always been a nation of creativity and perseverance; the bad news is we will have to find our way out of the darkness to become, again, that beacon of light to all of humanity. It's time to move forward. A unifying philosophy that we can all embrace as we seek traction is the common good. A belief in the common good of humanity would transcend differences in socioeconomic status, gender, religion, ethnic background, politics, and geography. It is the belief that good is shared among people or members of a society. It is the belief that the basic needs of the people in a society should and *must* be met.

Now, before someone starts yelling socialism, I say not so. I say, it's capitalism on steroids. This is especially true since more people, if the common good were advanced, would have the opportunity to participate in free enterprise. The vision would be to create a society where there is a bottom floor to prevent those at the bottom of the economic spectrum from falling through. In other words, we would meet the basic needs of each person—with his help, of course. Personal accountability has to be a factor. However, we should not limit a person's success. So, there is no ceiling—just a level playing field and an equal opportunity.

Now wait before you say, "Isn't that how it works now? That's why we have a safety net, right?" Let me remind you that far too many who were already at the bottom fell through that safety net when the economy bottomed out in 2008. Many others found themselves barely hanging on. Although the country is out of the recession, with unemployment down and the private sector adding jobs, it is true that not enough Americans *feel* the recovery. In fact, some incomes are lower coming out of this recession because of the lower-paying wages of the jobs added. The inaction of the US Congress to pass meaningful legislation to increase the minimum wage and create jobs is disheartening.

Nevertheless, true transformation and wholehearted commitment to the common good for all begins within the heart of the individual. I believe the intention to do good inherently lives within each of us, all of us. I refer to it as Spirit. Notice that whenever there has been a horrific event in our nation—such as 9/11 or Hurricane Katrina—a spiritual presence brings out that good intention. People automatically reach out to others in need during these times—even risking their own lives. There is no political element that drives the response, just the goodness, or Spirit, that exists within each of us. Yes, it's there, and it feels great when we can tap into that place in our hearts. Well, imagine what it would be like to live in that state of generosity and live with a constant outpouring of love.

I believe that a nation as great as our nation can only stay great if we are committed to the common good. Our nation has overcome slavery and the Great Depression; we have fought to see the implementation of civil rights, voting rights, Social Security, Medicare, and now the Affordable Care Act. In fact, we are a much better nation because of these triumphs. We must have learned something from these achievements.

We have always overcome tribulations and sided with the common good of the people. It was never easy, but it was necessary, and we were resilient. It took a lot of heart and a lot of hard work. But those days are gone, and now it's time for new transformation—imbued with the same heart and resilience we identify in our ancestors. The people of America have often set the stage for a change in policy. When people have demanded change for the common good, the government has often responded. In so many ways, we have reached a directional crossroads called Complacency Boulevard, and I believe the common good will prevail as it has in the past.

But change is difficult. Although we are innately born without judgment or condemnation, life experiences and the surrounding environment can make us uncaring and insensitive to others. The spirit of fear—not love—becomes the norm. But we are here on this earth at this moment in time for a reason.

So then, just how do we become the beings we were created to be in order to make the world a better place? The common good of humanity is a belief in the brotherhood of mankind. It is an awakening and a knowing that we *are* our brother's keeper—in the best of times and in the worst of times. Belief in the common good brings out the best in us as humans. If we believe in this principle, then it will be impossible to allow people to die in the richest country in the world simply because they could not afford, or did not have access to, healthcare or mental health treatment; and it would also be impossible to allow any child to go to bed hungry. Yet this happens in this country all too often.

Yes, what America needs now more than ever is a grassroots movement toward the common good, but that movement has to begin with each one of us: **one heart, one mind, one thought at a time**. Regardless of our backgrounds or our genetic makeup, there is good in everyone. We will not always agree. In fact, it is our differences that make our nation so beautiful and rich with diversity. However, the sheer beauty of the rainbow, much like the beauty of the diversity, cannot be celebrated if we do not open our minds and hearts to the beauty. We must live in a state of spiritual awareness, with a loving heart for all of God's people.

Much divides us as a people when it comes to our views on politics, race, religion, and sexual orientation—especially the growing inequalities that exist between the rich and the poor. Even so, we owe it to our children, our children's children, and to this great nation to focus on what we can do as individuals, as communities, and as a people to build something that will last.

If we are talking *at* each other and not *to* each other, it's hard to be heard. We have to learn how to coexist on the same planet, with an awareness that we are all connected. Truly, we will each ultimately be affected by whatever acts are occurring in this country and even the world. Our shared sense of responsibility is global.

Many will see the world based on the evening news or through the prism of their experiences. What we have seen or experienced will, in turn, impact our beliefs. Our beliefs inevitably shape the lives that we live. But learning is a lifelong journey, and when we know better, we can do better. Tomorrow we will learn something that we did not know today, and with an open heart, we will gain understanding.

Consider Proverbs 2:6, 9-11: "For the Lord gives wisdom; from his mouth come knowledge and understanding. . . . Then you will understand what is right and just and fair—every good path. For wisdom will enter your heart, and knowledge will be pleasant to your soul. Discretion will protect you, and understanding will guard you."

Because we have all had different experiences, the beliefs we hold may be different, but what is true and universal is that each of us has a purpose on this earth and holds a unique and important contribution to humanity. Each person is born into this world to do something great, each holding a gift, a purpose, and the missing piece of a gigantic puzzle. While some are busy with self-gratification at whatever cost that brings to the rest of the world, there are many others who spend their lives making monumental sacrifices and using their sacred gifts to make the world a better place. They are hard at work, building bridges and changing the lives of others each and every day. They each have a story.

These stories of ordinary individuals doing extraordinary things for the sake of the common good may not draw the attention of the media networks, which often broadcast grim stories that drive the highest network ratings. But the truth is that people all over the world are making a positive difference each and every day. I am talking about ordinary people doing extraordinary things. They truly are our unsung heroes. Many would like to pretend the unsung heroes do not exist, leading us instead to focus on what is not working in our country. Somehow, it is much easier to complain about the problems if we convince ourselves that no one is doing anything because everyone has given up. Somehow this thought brings solace.

Nevertheless, unsung heroes believe they have found their purpose. They have a growing understanding as to why they are here on this earth, and their understanding of this existence grows clearer as time passes. But we *all* have a purpose for being on this earth, and each of us has a unique gift that is the missing link to some of the most pressing issues in today's society.

No single person has all the answers, but in unity, as we work toward the common good, we can all be a part of the solution. The Dreamers, the Dream Defenders, and the Black Youth Project are all part of a growing culture of movements for change and empowerment. The work of the Innocence Project, through the use of DNA, is freeing those who were wrongly convicted many years ago and sentenced to death or life in prison. These examples show progress, and I do believe we are on the verge of something even bigger, a transformation that will change the nation and perhaps the world. A new dawn is rising!

Acknowledgments

To my mother and father, you raised me with the deepest and strongest love to be all that I am.

To my grandparents, you were my village.

To my brother, you inspired me never to give up.

To family, friends, and many others whom I have met along the journey, you have touched my life in so many ways. Thank you, and God bless.

Introduction

Transformation begins with complete self-examination. Go ahead and grab a mirror. I'll wait. Now start by looking in the mirror asking yourself these questions: What have I learned on my life's journey? How have these lessons shaped the life I now live? How have my experiences influenced my view of the world? Am I living on purpose, and what do I believe my purpose is? Do I have inner peace? What is my understanding of humanity, other cultures, and how we are all connected?

These are questions many have asked—or at least thought about. It is my prayer that this book will inspire you to look deep within and ask each of these questions. I hope you will carefully consider why you have come to believe as you do, and what you would like your personal footprint to be. Think of the part you were created to play in making this world a better place. Our greatest personal treasures may lie within the answers to these questions. Our answers may inspire a cooperative unleashing of potential.

Often I've heard religious leaders say, "We live in an evil world." Certainly, many evil acts are committed around the world, and these acts come from a place of fear that lives within. But is the world evil? There are many loving acts that occur each and every day, so could we also say, "We live in a loving world"? Sadly, I think if someone said that our world is loving, people might think he was disconnected from reality. But do our thoughts begin to shape a society? Does one evil act negate all the good that is done?

The point that I am trying to make is that if we believe the world is evil, then we expect evil and will, therefore, attract evil and live life looking through that prism. How we see the world will make a difference as to whether or not we can change it. However, the shaping of a society begins from the inside out: one heart, one mind, one thought at a time.

We live in what we believe is the greatest nation on earth, yet far too many in our country who go to work every day still live in poverty. We have the most obese nation in the industrialized world, yet far too many children are without food. Nevertheless, every day, people lose their lives trying to reach the shores of this great nation. So what makes a country great anyway? Immigrants come to America for a chance to live the American Dream. They are looking for the American Dream that many Americans feel they have lost. But is striving for the American Dream enough anymore? Or are we all being called to a higher purpose instead?

This book takes you on a journey with an author who believes that it *is* possible to transform a nation and the world, one heart, one mind, one thought at a time.

Your Belief Really Does Matter

The new year of 1992 was fast approaching, and I had decided to watch my alma mater, East Carolina University, play in the Peach Bowl in Atlanta, Georgia. The highways were filled with cars traveling to Atlanta, the purple and gold colors that decorated them, very telling. There was much excitement and much anticipation for the weekend, so sleep was not an option. On Saturday morning, there would be shopping and on Saturday evening, a good dinner and catching up with former college classmates. On Saturday night, we would go to Underground Atlanta, along with over a million others, to watch the giant peach drop at midnight in celebration of the new year coming in.

Before we knew it, it was time for the big event: the game. The day started out with a great breakfast, and we eventually made our way to the football stadium. East Carolina was considered the underdog, and it wasn't long before I knew why. North Carolina State University was killing us. Family and friends were watching it all on television back home in Virginia. We soon noticed that ECU fans were beginning to leave the stadium. After all, we were down by *three* touchdowns, and only *six* minutes were left in the game. We even began discussing whether *we* should leave and get a jump start on traffic.

However, we decided to stay a while longer. Feeling very disappointed, we looked to our left, and off at a distance, we could see a young man standing up in the stands. It was difficult to hear what he was yelling, but he was pointing to the team on the field, waving the gold foam sword (part of the pirate's costume for the school's mascot). I remember thinking he was probably just as angry and disappointed as the rest of us. However, it wasn't long before we could see that others around him had joined in, also waving their gold foam swords. I remember, at first, thinking, *What a waste of energy!* But then I was curious; they had my attention. Soon, it became much clearer what they were saying. The words, "I believe, I believe, I believe," were being chanted to the ECU players out on the field. Before long, this movement spread through the stadium, with ECU fans pointing the swords, or whatever they had in their hands, to the players on the field, chanting, "I believe, I believe, I believe." We joined in.

Then there was a moment that I will never forget. It seemed like time just stood still. Our players on the field looked up from the huddle into the stadium as we continued chanting, "I believe, I believe, I believe." There seemed to be what I describe now as a transfer of "energy." The fans' energy was slowly being transmitted to the players on the field. I can imagine that this must sound like hocus-pocus, and if I had not witnessed this firsthand, I, too, would be in disbelief. But I watched as the players prepared for their next play on the field. With six minutes left in the game, there it was: a perfect play and a touchdown, then another touchdown. Whew! Our heads were spinning. Two touchdowns, just like that! And with only seconds left in the game, there was a third touchdown!

We had come from behind, as the underdog, and scored three touchdowns in six minutes. We won the game: East Carolina University, 37, and North Carolina State, 34. Those numbers are still engrained in my head and also engraved on a sweatshirt that I purchased after the game. But it's my purple button with the words "I believe" printed in gold that I treasure the most. Friends and family watching this game on TV said that it was the best and most exciting game on TV that New Year's Day.

Over the years, I have thought about the course of events over and over in my mind, but the narrative is still the same. Someone stood up—alone at first—and stood firm in his belief. Others around him began to follow along, joining in like what is often seen in herd mentality. A movement was started. But, most importantly, it caught the attention of the players on the field. The players on the field felt the energy of the believers—and it was a game-changer!

This story tells us so much about what happens in life. Notice how fans had started to leave the game before it was over, believing it was impossible to come back and win. The same is true in life. Many will give up on our nation and simply stop believing. They will see defeat instead of seeing possibility or opportunity. But some will hold on to their faith and see the opportunity, the dream.

If we had left the game early that day, we would have never been part of that history-defining moment. More crucial still, if that young man had not stood up and stood firm in his belief, we may have never known what was possible. Humans function with a herd mentality and tend to flock like sheep and birds. Herd mentality describes how the behavior of people is influenced by others. Often, it leads to negative and irresponsible behavior, but it can also lead to positive behavior that can change the lives of others. This can be applied to all areas of life—from following the latest trends, the latest fashions, to the stock market trends. There have been many studies over time, analyzing human behavior and why humans react with herd mentality. But here is what I know for sure: We breathe the same air. We are all connected to one Source, one God, and when we move in unison, change can happen.

When we look at the great leaders of the world, namely those who were able to transform nations and who have had a lasting impact, Nelson Mandela, Dr. Martin Luther King Jr., and Mahatma Gandhi all come to mind. It is true that they all were great leaders in their time, but how did each person change the consciousness of a society to create a movement? How could they accomplish what so many could not? What do great leaders have in common?

So exactly what did a South African, an American, and an Indian have in common? They were from different countries and practiced different religions, but these leaders all had great faith and conviction and were willing to make monumental personal sacrifices. They put others before themselves and were guided by love and the common good.

I believe each one of us is called to greatness, and greatness is achieved through our personal journey. We are not born into the world with evil intentions, nor are we born with hatred or prejudice. What difference would it make if we could actually see the presence of God in everyone—no matter how deep we had to look? I mean, what if we could see though all the heartache, anger, arrogance, fear, and pain that has covered the light that exists in every human being? Even though babies are not born "evil," their learned behavior begins at an early age; some studies say it begins as newborns. Infants can, perhaps, take on the energy and the beliefs and the thoughts of others around them. Certainly, *we* can feel the difference between negative energy and positive energy that surrounds us on a daily basis, so maybe babies can too. If you surround yourself with negative people, day in and day out, that negative energy is absorbed into your system. Sooner or later, you become the product of that environment. On the other hand, if you are surrounded by kindness, love, and compassion, you will tend to project the same kindness, love, and compassion to others.

For every evil act, there are many acts of kindness. While we understand there are evil acts that happen on a daily basis—and we must be diligent about fighting for justice—we also know that acts of kindness take place every day, all over the world. It is my hope that we can begin to change the world by how we think. We attract positive or negative influences to our lives based on our intentions and beliefs. I once had a friend say that he always believed that he was going to get mugged; he just knew it. Well, guess what happened? Yes! That's exactly what happened one day: He got mugged.

However, if we change how we see things and add a positive spin to how we look at the world, then the things around us will change for the better. We must combat evil and fight for justice while, at the same time, using the most powerful weapon of all: love.

Once, when I was traveling, I was taking a flight back home and was really tired. I was also stressed out because my first flight was delayed, and I was not sure that I was going to make my connecting flight. There was an elderly lady sitting behind me who apparently could not speak English. I saw the flight attendant escort her to her seat when we boarded the plane. When the plane landed, all the passengers jumped up and started grabbing their luggage from the overhead bins, wanting to rush off the plane to get to their connecting flights. I am sure that many of them were in the same situation that I was in, wanting to make sure that they did not miss their next flights.

I also stood up and reached for my luggage in the overhead bin, but then I noticed the elderly lady sitting behind me was just sitting there, looking around and appearing very nervous. I caught her eye and offered a smile as I stood in the aisle, waiting to exit the plane. A few seconds later, after I had turned my back, I felt a light tap on my shoulder. I turned around, only to find her showing me her airline ticket and pointing to the ticket. She was speaking, but I could not understand a word she was saying. Although I could not understand her, I had a feeling she was trying to ask me what she should do and where she should go to make her connecting flight. I motioned for her to follow me off the plane, and she did. As we exited the plane, I found an airline attendant who could make sure she made her connecting flight. I knew that I had a very short time before my next flight was scheduled to leave, but I was not going to leave her without knowing someone was definitely going to help her.

I thought about this for the rest of the day. This lady only knew me through a smile, and although we had not sat together and there were many others around her, she felt comfortable enough to choose me. People come into our lives for many reasons, but everyone who comes into your life is there to teach you something. That day, she reminded me of the importance of a smile and how something so simple can speak volumes. A smile is a "universal language." Funny how such a small act can make a "world" of difference.

Each of us, through our faith, is connected to a Power, a Source, that is greater than we are. This higher power becomes the light in the face of darkness; it is our Creator. We are all connected to the Creator, a God who gives life. However, if in our journey we start to move away from that Source—especially during some of life's greatest challenges—we will begin to feel out of sorts, and it is much like moving away from light into darkness.

It's like a drop of water removed from the ocean. The ocean is the source for the drop of water. A single drop of water will eventually dry up if removed from the ocean. In life, without our Source, we start to lose hope, and sometimes even develop an addiction as a way of coping. On the other hand, the more we feel connected to our source, the more we are able to feel life and love, which can be transmitted to others through us. Living a more consciously aware and spiritually connected life will change how we look at things, allowing us a more merciful outlook on those around us. When we change how we look at things, the things around us start to change. Even quantum physics supports this!

Along the way, we will always face the weariness test. Galatians 6:9 says, "Let us not become weary in doing good, for at the proper time we will reap a harvest if we do not give up." America may seem weary now, which makes us see the problems instead of the possibilities, but life is full of just as many possibilities as problems. So, if you don't like what you see, turn the channel, and look at the situation differently.

This book takes you on a journey to meet ordinary people and observe their extraordinary lives. In his own way, each of these individuals is using spiritual gifts to change the nation. If we live life in a bubble, we will only get to know the people in our immediate sphere and have predictable conversations in our limited social circles. Thus, we miss out on a great opportunity. Sadly, there are many reasons we simply don't get to know others we see as "different."

Chapter 1 in this book examines the economy and the state of the nation—a divided government, widespread poverty, and growing income disparity define America today. Chapter 2 discusses how our experiences at an early age shape our thoughts and impact our decisions as we grow older; it also explores a journey of spirituality. Chapter 3 introduces ordinary people who are making a difference. Chapter 4 takes a look at the Millennial Generation and how the millennials are already creating change and opportunities for this generation to make a "world" of difference. Chapter 5 deals with social entrepreneurship and what can be seen as a merging of the conscience and our business practices to create enterprises that are impacting communities around the country and the world. We end with Chapter 6 and a discussion about the importance of relationships—the foundation for healthy business, political, and religious communities. Indeed, relationships are our cornerstone as we build a future for the common good.

CHAPTER 1

It's Not Just the Economy

"Rediscovering Lost Values" (1954, Sermon)

Man's scientific genius has been amazing. I think we have to look much deeper than that if we are to find the real cause of man's problems and the real cause of the world's ills today. If we are to really find it I think we will have to look in the hearts and souls of men. The trouble isn't so much that we don't know enough, but it's as if we aren't good enough. The trouble isn't so much that our scientific genius lags behind, but our moral genius lags behind. The great problem facing modern man is that, that the means by which we live, have outdistanced the spiritual ends for which we live. So we find ourselves caught in a messed-up world. The problem is with man himself and man's soul. We haven't learned how to

be just and honest and kind and true and loving. And that is the basis of
our problem. The real problem is that through our scientific genius we've
made of the world a neighborhood, but through our moral and spiritual
genius we've failed to make of it a brotherhood. [1]

—Dr. Martin Luther King Jr.

Economic or Moral Crisis?

It's not just the economy that has America off course. Rather, there is a very disturbing, underlying problem that we face as a nation. In 2009, we experienced the most devastating economic downfall since the Great Depression in the 1930s. We were losing nearly 800,000 jobs per month in this country. The stock market plummeted. People lost their life savings, lost their homes, and gained a sense of despair that most had never seen. We could talk about the economic crisis and how we got there, but I believe there is a more disturbing crisis at hand. We must examine a much deeper problem: the moral crisis. The economic crisis is the symptom of the underlying moral problem.

The moral crisis is like a cancer left untreated. To make sense out of this, we have to examine a few things. We are the wealthiest country in the world, yet 48 million persons in this country were without health insurance in 2012.[2] (The number has started to decline as a result of the Affordable Healthcare Act.) We throw away nearly 40 percent of our food according to a report released by the Natural Resource Defense Council. Considering the resources to grow and produce the food, this would be worth more than $165 billion annually for food that never gets eaten.[3] This is even more difficult to reconcile when you look at the statistics on food insecurity. According to the US Department of Agriculture report, "Household Food Security in the United States in 2013," 85.7 percent of American households were food secure throughout 2013, leaving 14.3 percent of households food insecure at least some time during the year, including 5.6 percent with very low food security.[4] Food insecurity means there is not enough food in the household for all members of the family to eat three meals a day, and food consumption is reduced because of a lack of money and other resources needed to access food. Often this means stretching the meals to make them last longer. Children were food insecure at times during the year in 9.9 percent of households with children, or 3.8 million households total. These households were unable, at times during the year, to provide adequate, nutritious meals for their children. Rates of food insecurity were substantially higher than the national average for households with incomes near or below the Federal Poverty Level, households with children headed by single women or single men, and black and Hispanic households. Food insecurity was more common in large cities and rural areas than in suburban areas and other outlying areas around large cities.[5] We are the most obese nation in the industrialized world, and while we have an obesity problem, at the same time, we also have a hunger problem.

We cannot sustain economic growth in this country when there is such a large disparity of income and wealth among our citizens. How can a country be so willing to leave so many behind? To put things in context, we have to look at the Great Depression. The peak of the Great Depression took place between 1932 and 1933. In the 1920s, prior to the Great Depression, the wealthiest 1 percent owned more than a third of American assets. The average income of the American family dropped by 40 percent from 1929 to 1932.

Fast-forward to the recent recession experienced in the United States, where economic inequality has continued to grow. Overall, incomes have declined even as job growth has occurred. I believe that addressing economic inequality is the key to economic growth. Although poverty rates have declined as a whole since the War on Poverty in the 1960s (in 1959, over 22 percent of Americans were living in poverty), a discouraging 15 percent of all Americans still live in poverty, according to the 2012 census data. That report shows 46.5 million people living at or below the poverty line. In 2012, 13.7 percent of people 18 to 64 were in poverty, compared with 9.1 percent of people 65 and older. But it is the 21.8 percent of children under 18, or 16.1 million, living in poverty that should have this country outraged.[6]

Although there has been some decline, resulting from the War on Poverty declared by US President Lyndon B. Johnson in the 1960s, the growing income inequality is concerning. Income inequality is the highest since the Depression, with the "richest 1% in the United States now owning more wealth than the bottom 90%."[7] In addition, the income inequality between women and men in the workplace is ever-present. In 2012 there was a 77 percent female-to-male earnings ratio. Therefore, women were only paid 77 cents for every one dollar that men earned when there were no differences in the job requirements.

A growing inequality in income is not healthy for our nation and threatens the overall health of our economy. Without a living wage, it is harder and harder for families to make ends meet. When income increases for those with lower wages, the money normally goes back into the economy through the purchasing of goods and services. Only those who have lived with blinders on, totally removed from the rest of the world, would fail to understand the consequences, turmoil, and instability that could result if, as a nation, we continue to ignore such a growing disparity. When people get up every day and go to work, only to find an eviction notice on the door at day's end, or when looking for a job becomes the full-time employment opportunity, there is something very sinister about this picture.

Nevertheless, the scenario is not new. Instability has existed in numerous countries because of income disparities and feeling disenfranchised from society. Egypt is one example that comes to mind. Some would say that the upheavals that led to the 2010-2011 protests by Egyptians were inevitable, due to the high unemployment, food price inflation, and low minimum wages there. So what can we learn from the Egyptian crisis? History has shown us, both in Egypt and in other societies, what happens when the rights and dignity of a people are ignored by denying citizens the opportunity to make a living wage.

A living wage is the minimum income a person would need in order to meet his basic needs; it merely keeps up with the cost of living. Many nations have fallen because of systems that devalued segments of their societies. I know that there are some who want to blame the growing numbers of children in poverty on the increase in the number of single-parent households. Indeed, 24 percent of the 75 million children under age 18 live in a single-mother family. Seven in 10 children living with a single mother are poor or low income—compared with less than a third of children living in other types of families.[8] Many single mothers already have two strikes against them. First, many lack a living wage. Second, just being a woman means receiving, on average, 77 cents to every dollar the male counterpart will receive in wages. For minority women, the gap is even greater.

America must be grounded on the laws of equal justice, freedom of speech and religion, and respect for all her people—not just some of her people.

My notion of democracy is that under it the weakest should have the same opportunity as the strongest.

—**Gandhi**

Poverty

Poverty is defined by Webster's Dictionary as a lack of a certain amount of material possessions or money. Absolute poverty, or destitution, is an inability to afford basic human needs, which commonly include clean and fresh water, nutrition, healthcare, education, clothing, and shelter. Today, about 1.7 billion people are estimated to live in absolute poverty around the world. Relative poverty, or economic inequality, refers to lacking a usual or socially acceptable level of resources or income as compared with others within a society or country. [9]

Global Perspective on Poverty

From a global perspective, the United Nations states, "Fundamentally, poverty is a denial of choices and opportunities, a violation of human dignity. It means lack of basic capacity to participate effectively in society. It means not having enough to feed and clothe a family, not having a school or clinic to go to, not having the land on which to grow one's food, a job to earn one's living, or not having access to credit. It means insecurity, powerlessness, and exclusion of individuals, households, and communities. It means susceptibility to violence, and it often implies living in marginal or fragile environments, without access to clean water or sanitation." [10]

The World Bank states, "Poverty is a pronounced deprivation in well-being and comprises many dimensions. It includes low incomes and the inability to acquire the basic goods and services necessary for survival with dignity. Poverty also encompasses low levels of health and education, poor access to clean water and sanitation, inadequate physical security, lack of voice, and insufficient capacity and opportunity to better one's life." [11]

According to UNICEF, in 2008, 8.8 million children worldwide died before their fifth birthdays, while one billion children were deprived of one or two of the essentials for survival and development. [12] This is consistent with the reports that over 20,000 children under five years old die around the world on a daily basis, mostly related to poverty and hunger.

Poverty is the worst form of violence.
—Gandhi

Poverty in America

As a consultant for the US Department of Health and Human Services (DHHS), I have spent time in many communities in this country—well over 200 cities in nearly 40 states. Seeing the struggle of local governments and communities trying to balance the needs of the people with the decisions that have been made at the state level—and sometimes at the federal level—has been challenging at best.

Many communities across the country were suffering from the decline in manufacturing well before the 2009 recession. At the turn of the twentieth century, the country was thriving in industry, but by the 1970s and 1980s, that started to change as other countries, such as Japan and China, seized the opportunity and started out-producing the United States. As thriving industries began to fold in communities all across our country, the closures left gaps in many of the communities. I grew up in a community where everyone worked at industrial plants, and when the plants closed, the community took a hit as workers lost their livelihoods.

As we reached the depths of our 2009 economic crisis in the United States, we saw income inequality continue to increase. This, of course, compounded a problem that already existed in many communities due to the decline in industry. The most recent data on poverty in America shows that the poor have gotten poorer and the rich have gotten richer. So what are the facts? Let's look more closely at poverty in America.

Poverty in America is real, but unnecessary. Poverty in America has been created by a lack of vision and the lack of representation for all Americans. Some have said that poverty is man-made. Most of those in poverty are working-class citizens. They have jobs and contribute to society, yet they do not make a living wage. What does it mean to be poor, and why should we care? And should our concern for poverty even extend beyond the walls of this great nation?

Poverty is not new in America. In March 1964, Lyndon B. Johnson launched the War on Poverty and wrote a letter to the United States Congress. Excerpts from the letter:

We are citizens of the richest and most fortunate nation in the history of the world.

One hundred and eighty years ago, we were a small country struggling for survival on the margin of a hostile land.

Today we have established a civilization of free men, which spans an entire continent.

With the growth of our country has come opportunity for our people—opportunity to educate our children, to use our energies in productive work, to increase our leisure-opportunity for almost every American to hope that through work and talent he could create a better life for himself and his family.

The path forward has not been an easy one.

But we have never lost sight of our goal: an America in which every citizen shares all the opportunities of his society, in which every man has a chance to advance his welfare to the limit of his capacities.

We have come a long way toward this goal.

We still have a long way to go.

The distance which remains is the measure of the great unfinished work of our society. To finish that work I have called for a national war on poverty . . . the young man or woman who grows up without a decent education, in a broken home, in a hostile and squalid environment, in ill health or in the face of racial injustice- that young man or woman is often trapped in a life of poverty.[13]

The implementation of social programs, including Social Security, Medicare, and Medicaid, has helped many Americans in poverty. Although poverty has fallen for African Americans since

1964, African Americans still have some of the greatest poverty rates in the country. In 2012, 12.7 percent of whites lived in poverty, but for African Americans, that number was 27.2 percent (down from 42 percent in 1966) and for Hispanics, it was 25.6 percent (up from 22.8 percent in 1972). [14]

However, I think most will agree that child poverty is the greatest concern. According to the American Community Survey Brief (ACS), "More than one in five children in the United States (15.75 million) lived in poverty in 2010. The 2010 ACS child poverty rate (21.6 percent) is the highest since the survey began in 2001. For children identified as Black the poverty rate was 38.2 percent (4.0 million), twice as high as the rate for White children and the highest poverty rate among the race and ethnic groups presented in this report" [15]

On March 31, 1968, a few days before his death on April 4 of that year, Dr. Martin Luther King spoke on poverty at the National Cathedral in Washington, DC. At the time, he was in the process of planning and organizing The Poor People's Campaign to end poverty by creating jobs, improving housing, and raising income for all those living in poverty. In his speech "Remaining Awake through a Great Revolution," Dr. King stated that "in addition to racial injustice, poverty and war are two 'evils' that must be addressed." The Poor People's Campaign march was scheduled for May 1968, but King was killed in Memphis, Tennessee, just one month prior to the march. One of the places Dr. King had traveled previously was Marks, Mississippi, in Quitman County, which he referenced in his speech. This was the home to The Poor People's Campaign. He called it the poorest county in the United States at the time. This area of the country is known as the Mississippi Delta, an area I have traveled to a few times. While 15.8 percent or 48.8 million

Americans lived in poverty in 2013[16], in 2012 in Mississippi, the figure was 22.8 percent, and in some areas in the Mississippi Delta, like Leflore County, the poverty level was upwards of 45.3 percent of the population living in poverty, and for children, from birth to age 17, it was reported as high as 62.3 percent. [17]

Where is the safety net for these communities? What have we learned in the last few decades about protecting our most vulnerable populations: the elderly, our children, the poor? Have we gotten better as a country when it comes to protecting our most vulnerable? After Hurricane Katrina, many were certain we would see change that would include a grassroots movement and better collaboration, between local, state, and federal governments and these struggling communities, to build a safety net. Although some progress has been made, we still have a ways to go.

Many of the residents affected by Katrina, especially in New Orleans, did not have the means or the transportation to evacuate the city; furthermore, the infrastructure was not in place to facilitate such an evacuation. So the systems failed miserably, and people lost their lives. Many would say, "People are where they are because of the choices they have made." I absolutely agree that many have made choices in their lives that have resulted in less than optimal situations, but shouldn't we want a society where everyone has the opportunity to propel themselves upward- not some but all? Studies have shown that, in the United States, if you are born in poverty, there is a generational element, and it is likely you will stay in poverty. Upward mobility is challenging. This makes it even more difficult to break the cycle of poverty.

Do we have the will to overcome the odds and make the necessary changes in our country to protect our most vulnerable populations?

I think the most important question is this: What will be the consequences if we don't? Of course, this is a humanitarian issue, but it is also the disease of immorality, with symptoms of economic inequality. The growing disparity in America threatens the very fabric of our country.

All great things are simple, and many can be expressed in single words: freedom, justice, honor, duty, mercy, hope.

—Winston Churchill

Economics and Health

The economics in a community can greatly impact the health of the community and will determine the community members' access to healthcare. This is why the Affordable Care Act is so important for many Americans. Countless citizens have had to choose between healthcare and putting food on the table—literally. The problem is that the uninsured end up in hospital emergency rooms, where charges exceed what a doctor's visit would cost. Well, you can believe that someone will end up paying for that bill in the ER, and this has always been the case. The cost to treat the uninsured being seen in hospitals will get shifted to insurance companies, and the cost will eventually raise the cost of premiums for all those who have insurance. This is known as "cost shifting" in the healthcare industry and has been the normal practice. It is difficult to ignore a problem and not pay for it later.

There is, however, an unspoken "healthcare safety net" that, for decades, has served the uninsured and underinsured populations. I am speaking about Federally Qualified Health Centers (FQHCs).

There are FQHCs all across the country. These FQHCs as they are called, are subsidized by the federal government under Section 330 of the Public Health Service Act. Millions of Americans currently access these health centers for care in states across the country. Patients cannot be turned away based on their inability to pay, and any patient charges are based on an individual's income. This model of care has proven to be effective and has increased access to care for millions of Americans; it provides primary care for all age groups. The centers are required to serve Medically Underserved Areas (MUA) or Medically Underserved Populations (MUP), which must be designated as such by the federal government. There are also many other types of programs that benefit communities in rural and urban areas—just not enough.

If a community is economically disadvantaged, chances are that the health status of the community will be challenged as well. The incidents of cancer, diabetes, and heart disease are endemic in most communities of poverty. The federal government does, however, set goals for the health of our country. In 2010, the Department of Health and Human Services launched Healthy People 2020, an initiative with goals and objectives designed to improve the quality of life and eliminate healthcare disparities in the United States. These objectives are released every 10 years.

Take cancer, for example. The overall rate of death in 2010 was 172.8 per 100,000 persons on average (this number would vary based on types of cancer, etc.), but in some populations, such as African Americans, the number is 208 per 100,000. The goal for 2020 is to decrease that number to 160 per 100,000 persons. The rate of diabetes in various populations also varies a great deal.[18] "In 2010, 4.6% of the population were unable to obtain, or there was a delay in obtaining, necessary medical care. This rate varied by race and ethnicity as well as by family income. The same studies show that when it comes to diabetes, new cases of diabetes for adults drastically increase when a person is poor: 13.9 cases per 1,000 persons for people in poverty, versus 5.0 cases for persons at 600% above the poverty level."[19]

The research is very clear: There is a direct link between poverty and incidents of disease and death. It is still very difficult to imagine that in the wealthiest country in the world this could be the case. A study released in 2009 by David Cecere, Cambridge Health Alliance, linked 45,000 annual deaths with a lack of health insurance. The study analyzed data from the US Centers for Disease Control and Prevention (CDC) to assess the death rates. The analysis took into account education, income, and other factors, including smoking, drinking, and obesity. The study found a 40 percent increase in risk of death among the uninsured. A coauthor in the study, Dr. David Himmelstein, estimated that "one American dies every twelve minutes from lack of health insurance." This differs, he states, from the original estimate by the Institute of Medicine, which estimated one American dies every 30 minutes from lack of health insurance.[20]

We have the best innovation and research in health in the world. We spend almost 17 percent of the gross domestic product (GDP) on healthcare—more than any other country in the developed world. Nevertheless, according to a recent study by the National Institutes of Health and National Research Council, "U.S. Health in International Perspective: Shorter Lives, Poorer Health," "Americans die sooner and experience more illness than residents in many other countries. While the length of life has improved in the U.S., other countries have gained life years even faster . . . the U.S. health disadvantage is expressed in higher rates of chronic disease and mortality among adults and in higher rates of untimely death and injuries among adolescents and small children . . . the report describes multiple, plausible explanations, from deficiencies in the health system to high rates of unhealthy behaviors and from adverse social conditions to unhealthy environments."[21] Therefore, while economics may be a factor in health outcome, it is by no means the only factor.

Economics and Education

One might say that the way out of poverty is through a good education. However, the dropout rates within the public school system are staggering. In some states, high school dropout rates exceed 50 percent. Children coming from broken homes without strong family support systems are particularly at risk. Studies show that a child is most likely to complete school when someone shows an interest in that child. The action of a local National Association for the Advancement of Colored People (NAACP) organization resulted in improved grades for African-American boys in grades six through eight who had been tagged at-risk with failing grades. The president of the NAACP decided to take action when hearing about these boys.

The first step included inviting the pastors of predominantly African-American churches to a meeting held at one of the local churches. The meeting was to discuss potential opportunities for community involvement between the churches and the NAACP. I was asked to co-facilitate the initial meeting. The general consensus from those in attendance was that action needed to be taken, and all agreed that focusing on the youth would be a good place to start. Several meetings followed. The meetings that followed, led by a former educator, developed a mentorship program for the youth who were not performing academically. The group felt that most of the youth did not have positive male role models and that increasing the presence of role models would have a positive effect on the youth.

Plans were made for a kickoff meeting that would include 50 African-American men in the community from various professions; most were retired. The men planned to meet with the youth at this initial meeting to kick off what would be a series of meetings over the next couple of years. The objective of the experiment was not to tutor the youth, but to frame the possibility of opportunities for these young males. Quite often, young African-American boys who are underperforming in school will not have the opportunity to have such positive reinforcements or role models in their lives. Most of the mentors who participated in the program were retired professionals, so certainly this was a rewarding experience for them as well. The program was a success, with the school system reporting that the grades of these young men actually improved!

There is a link between poverty and education. "Powerful evidence of this link include the fact that 46 percent of Americans who grew up in low-income families but failed to earn college degrees stayed in the lowest income quintile, compared to 16 percent for those who earned a college degree." [22]

CHAPTER 2

Nothing for My Journey

We make a living by what we get, but we make a life by what we give.

—Winston Churchill

An individual has not started living until he can rise above the narrow confines of his individualistic concerns to the broader concerns of all humanity.

—Dr. Martin Luther King Jr.

A fundamental concern for others in our individual and community lives would go a long way in making the world the better place we so passionately dreamt of.
—**Nelson Mandela**

Dare to Dream

I believe that we are called to a higher purpose.
With every waking moment, the purpose lives on.
Open your heart and hear the whisper of the wind.
Calling . . . Calling.
Dare to dream!

You have broken all the rules, because you dared to dream.
When some said no way, you dared to dream.
When others said impossible, you dared to dream.
When some projected the life they thought you should live,
you dared to dream.

Many gave directions, but God controlled the compass
on the winding, sometimes rocky road.

Your journey was not bound by tradition or by the expectation of others.
It was freed by the spiritual presence of the "I am."
You found strength, but yet humility.

Many times veering off the busy highway to
Take the road less traveled . . .
Full of curves, unpaved and yet longer . . .

Every bump in the road drew you closer to God
and closer to your purpose.

Wouldn't take nothing for my Journey.

—Juanita Farrow

Religion and Spirituality

Both our experiences and beliefs impact how we see the world. The journey of our life is full of experiences, and those experiences can be transforming—even leading to a spiritual transformation. A spiritual transformation occurs in our journey to connect with our higher self—beyond the ego—and reach a higher consciousness. American psychologist Abraham Maslow called this self-actualization.

When I was in college, I was fascinated with psychology. I was especially drawn to the study of Maslow's hierarchy of human needs, the five-stage model. At the bottom of the pyramid is the most basic level of physiological needs, such as food, water, and shelter. At the top of the pyramid is self-actualization, or being able to realize the highest form of personal growth or self-fulfillment.

Certainly, change starts with what we believe, but it is rather our way of life, or our day-to-day walk according to our faith, that best characterizes who we are. Simply being religious is not enough. People can talk you in and out of theology, but people cannot talk you out of a personal relationship or experience with God. Your walk is based on a knowing in your soul.

Evil acts are committed all over the world—yes, even in the United States—in the name of religion. Consider what Dr. Myles

Munroe says about religion: "Religion is not a peaceful prospect. And religious conflict is not restricted to Islam or Hinduism or other 'non-Western' religions. Christianity carries its own heavy burden of responsibility for religiously motivated conflict. The Crusades of the Middle Ages and centuries of hostility and persecution between Catholics and Protestants are two prime examples. Think of all the years that Belfast and all Northern Ireland burned with unrest and violence because Catholics and Protestants were unable to live together in peace. Denominations within the Church are like little kingdoms of their own, jockeying for position and advantage and fighting amongst themselves over theology, doctrine . . . instead of working together for the common cause of the Gospel. This is why I make a clear and unambiguous distinction between the Kingdom of Heaven and institutional Christianity as a religious entity. They are not the same."[23]

Dr. King, a Christian and Baptist minister, was drawn to the idea of a nonviolent movement. Mahatma Gandhi's teachings were a great inspiration to Dr. King. King used Gandhi's successful nonviolent movement toward independence and social justice in India as inspiration during the Civil Rights Movement in the United States. Although Gandhi was Hindu and Dr. King was Christian, Dr. King effectively used Gandhi's movement of nonviolence with the Christian principles of love to create a powerful strategy in the Civil Rights Movement.

I grew up in rural America, in a small town that was very conservative and in a largely African-American community. What I remember most about church is perhaps something totally out of the ordinary. It was not so much the two Sundays a month "church experience" (in communities then, and even some today, Sunday school was held every Sunday but church services were only held two Sundays a month), but it was the spiritual experience that occurred *after* church. I can thank my grandmother for that experience. Maybe without realizing it, this was her way of demonstrating being religious but also being spiritual.

My grandmother is the best example I can give of the difference between church membership and spirit-filled discipleship. Grandmother was quiet and shy but spiritually bold in her actions. She was determined to make a difference in the lives of her grandchildren. Sometimes, it is common to feel powerless, as if there is no way you can make a difference in the world. I'm sure there were times when Grandmother felt the same way, but nevertheless she stood firm in her faith. She could not have known just how much she would change the lives of those around her, or the lasting impression she would have on the children in her life, especially her grandchildren. We were raised in a "village," and the experiences and lessons linger on.

I know what is possible by the examples I saw through her life. When I was just a child growing up in rural North Carolina, I would watch my grandparents and would listen intently when they talked because I knew they always had something to say to make me feel better. My grandmother passed away when I was just 15 years old, and my grandfather had passed away five years before. I was very close to my grandparents and spent a lot of time with them while my parents worked. Grandmother was an active churchgoer and children's Sunday school teacher. She had a humble and quiet spirit. I never knew her even to raise her voice, but yet in such a quiet way, she exhibited quite a bit of influence and power. She was somewhat of a pioneer in her time. Although I could not truly understand this at that time, it is very clear now that she must have felt this inner nudging inside to be different, to think outside the box. With Grandmother, it was all about what she could do for others. That's what our time on earth is about: service. She became a living vessel and allowed herself to be used and to become an instrument of love. She was referred to as the "mother of the church," a title used to recognize the elderly mother of the church who had exhibited commitment and leadership.

In addition to teaching Sunday school, Grandmother led a children's church group called the "Sunshine Band," where children learned about leadership, held office positions, had meetings, and traveled the state. You would think that she would have been content as a grandmother, mother of the church, Sunday school teacher, and director of the Sunshine Band; however, that was just the tip of the iceberg. She woke up every Sunday morning very early. If the children in her Sunday school class did not have transportation to get to church, she took it upon herself—even if it meant making several trips back and forth to church on Sunday morning, picking up the children to attend her class. Transportation to church did not exist then as it does today. After church was out, she made sure each child had a ride back home before she headed out. Now, that's enough to make anyone feel like she's put in a good day's work. But most surprisingly, it was not what she did *in* church, but what she did *outside* of church that would become her legacy in her purpose-driven life.

You see, Sundays after church meant family gatherings at Grandmother's house. You could smell the fried chicken cooking in the kitchen, but most of the family gathered around my aunt playing the piano in the living room. Songs of worship and praise filled the air. This was family time. But it wasn't long before the community took note. Some began to gather on the front lawn or the porch— wherever there was space. They were just curious at first; it was quite different from traditional church, and it really did not seem much like church. They walked for miles down the dusty gravel road. They came for the fellowship, prayers, testimonies, singing, and the anointing that took place—not to mention Grandmother's fried chicken.

The gathering was lively, never boring, and always seemed to make people feel better. There were some who suffered from mental illness, some from substance abuse, and some were just lonely. Grandmother was never stuck on labels, but she *was* stuck on making a difference in the lives of people. From the highway to a dusty gravel road that seemed to stretch for miles, that's how far people walked to get to her house. Those who were brokenhearted, those who felt rejected by society or rejected by the traditional church—they all came. She never turned anyone way, and although she did not have a lot of money, she managed to feed everyone who came. Forty years later, the people who grew up in that small community still talk about how she impacted their lives and the lives of many others. She made them feel whole, special.

It's only now that I understand she had to be driven by something much bigger than herself. If she had never walked in her faith, think about the lives she might not have impacted. Although too young to recognize it back then, I now know that her actions demonstrated something that was great. She took the extra steps to do what she felt was necessary to reach people where they were. A person in his or her brokenheartedness may not feel worthy or may have difficulty believing he is created in God's perfect image. Feeling beat down by life, many do not feel comfortable in the traditional church. Afraid they will be judged or will not fit in, they choose not to go. Grandmother's actions showed a younger generation something that was profound. There was no judgment or condemnation—just lots of broken souls in need of a spiritual healing. The message was simple, but it was effective.

Yes, she was different, and while others may have disagreed with her, it never stopped her from believing she could make a difference. Maybe she did figure out that she really could change the world, *her world*, one person at a time. If that simple message is being carried on 40 years later, then her legacy is still making a difference in the lives of many! I don't even think that Grandmother knew how many lives she changed—all because she became a vessel and allowed unconditional love to flow within. She chose not be bound by tradition, but to live on purpose instead.

We often travel through life on automatic pilot and fail to live consciously. We see the world through the lens of the media and sometimes feel hopeless to make a difference. But the truth of the matter is that there are many "on the battlefield" making a difference around the world; we just need more of them.

Gandhi once spoke of religion by saying, "You must watch my life, how I eat, sit, talk, behave in general. The sum total of all those in me is my religion."

Christians are members of the universal body of Christ—not because of identification with the institution of the church, but through identification with Christ directly, through faith. So if we see the church as a living, breathing organism and not brick and mortar, then we begin to understand that we are spiritual beings in this world having a human experience. The church has often been the staple of communities, especially the African-American community. As I've traveled throughout the country and, in many cases, to some of the most poverty-stricken communities, there seems to be a disconnect between the institution of the church and the community. What if all churches were united for the common good?

However, even more prevalent is what is happening in Washington politics. Never before have I heard more about Christianity and faith than what is currently espoused by our members in Congress and the media. Many openly talk about their faith and the role that their religion plays in their own lives. But wait, are there not congressional members who have introduced legislation that would severely impact some of the poorest in the country? On January 27, 2014, the *New York Times* reported the House and Senate negotiators agreed on a five-year farm bill, cutting eight billion dollars from the Supplemental Nutrition Assistance Program (SNAP)/ Food Assistance Program over the next decade.[24] The program, which is a safety net for the most venerable population and children, is being cut at a time when hunger is still very much a problem in the United States. Is this a faith strategy of some sort? Then there has been discussion to introduce legislation that would cut the program even further, gutting over 40 billion dollars from it. I cannot even imagine the impact that this would have on some of the neediest in the country. The program was introduced in the 1970s to alleviate and prevent malnutrition in our country. How is it that we can ignore the numbers—of children especially—who will be impacted by such decisions? Somehow this sends a very strong message. Many times what we are willing to do speaks louder than what we say we believe.

Faith is an action. It is a response to something. This leads to this question: Can you have faith without action? Does the United States of America still consider itself one of the most Christian societies in the world? The country was founded on Christian principles. So how do we reconcile faith and the actions of this country, or the willingness to leave fellow Americans, our brothers and sisters, behind? I mean, I am not referring to a handout, just a hand up.

I reviewed a study recently that was conducted to look at religion versus spirituality in the church. I remember the results of that survey, as it is something I have not been able to get out of my mind. The survey results revealed that, on average, church members were "religious," but not "spiritual." This was almost 20 years ago, and I know that part of my own spiritual journey has been to understand or feel the difference. I did not go out actively seeking to understand; however on my own journey, I do believe I have become more conscious that there is a difference.

Religion is defined as an organized system of beliefs and rules used or practiced. Worship is the most basic element of the practice of one's belief. Spirituality is an experience or feeling of unconditional love; it's God's call within your soul. This "knowing" of unconditional love comes from a relationship with a higher power or presence in one's life. Some religious leaders say that Christianity, for example, was never meant to be a religion since a religion is based on laws and rules and the core principle of Christianity is the *relationship* with Christ. Yes, it is the relationship that matters. Without the relationship with a higher power, it is easy to make decisions that impact the most vulnerable populations—without thinking twice about the impact.

Once we have the relationship, we *know* that we *are* our brother's keeper. It becomes essential, as individuals, as a community, and as a nation, to do what is right. The government will then be seen as a partner and not the enemy and will pass meaningful legislation that supports the common good for our country. We will be able to lift people out of poverty using a sound and aggressive economic strategy, including a living wage, job creation, and targeted programs for the most impoverished communities. But don't take my word for it. Let's consider what Christ said.

The Beatitudes were presented by Jesus in what is now known as the Sermon on the Mount. In this teaching, Jesus offers us a way of life that promises eternity in the Kingdom of Heaven. The Ten Commandments were given to Moses on Mount Sinai in the Old Testament book of Exodus; these commands stressed what "thou shalt not" do in this life on earth. This was the Law. However, the Beatitudes in the Gospel of Matthew present a message of humility, charity, and brotherly love. The Beatitudes echo Jesus's teachings on spirituality, compassion, and mercy. It is a message based on love: our love for each other and our love of mankind. It is a guide for spiritual growth, showing how to build bridges of transformation and obtain real joy in the middle of the storm. Jesus took his disciples and sat down and taught them these crucial principles concerning love and service.

The Eight Beatitudes of Jesus
(Gospel of St. Matthew 5:3-10 KJV)

"Blessed are the poor in spirit: for theirs is the kingdom of heaven."

Blessed in each of the verses means *happy*. Poor in spirit is to have a broken spirit. One can have all the riches in the world and still have a broken spirit or be spiritually poor. So, when you feel beat down by the world or overburdened and you just feel like giving up, Jesus said, "Come unto me, all ye that labour and are heavy laden, and I will give you rest." (Matthew 11:28 KJV) God does not despise a broken spirit because of his infinite compassion, mercy, and grace, which is promised to all those who are broken-spirited. This is the same compassion and mercy he expects man to show to his brethren.

"Blessed are they that mourn: for they shall be comforted."

Those who mourn are those with a penitent spirit. We should mourn or be sad for the suffering of others and mourn for those we have hurt. Mourning allows us to grow in love and be comforted by the Holy Spirit. Also, when we feel or exhibit remorse for our misdeeds, this will open our hearts to the grace and mercy that God has already afforded us. The Holy Spirit was left as a comforter for each of us if we only believe and have faith.

"Blessed are the meek: for they shall inherit the earth."

Those who are meek are mild-tempered, gentle-spirited. Even with our differences and in times when we do not agree, Jesus tells us to be meek. When a person is mild-tempered and gentle-spirited, he has the same character as Jesus. Consider Matthew 11:29: "Take my yoke upon you and learn of me, for I am meek and lowly in heart: and ye shall find rest unto your souls." Jesus teaches that when we are kind and gentle, we shall inherit the earth. Jesus inherited the earth, and we can share in this inheritance.

"Blessed are they which do hunger and thirst after righteousness: for they shall be filled."

Happy are those who hunger and thirst for righteousness or seek God and desire to be fed by His Word through the

Holy Spirit. When you seek God for knowledge, wisdom, and understanding, He will deliver. The thirst is for divine righteousness—not self-righteousness. God will put people in your life to help you learn and understand the meaning of his Word. "God is a Spirit: and they that worship him must worship him in spirit and in truth." (John 4:24 KJV) We should have the desire in our hearts for justice for all. There must be a burning passion and the courage inside each of us to stand up for justice for all of God's people.

"Blessed are the merciful: for they shall obtain mercy."

Being merciful is having a compassionate and forgiving spirit. We must be compassionate to one another and willing to show each other kindness. Our Heavenly Father is merciful with us, and we must be merciful toward others. Acts of mercy provide spiritual benefit, demonstrating love and compassion for everyone and forgiveness toward those who have hurt us. Seek reconciliation. Love thy neighbor. Jesus even speaks of this by saying, "For I was hungry and you fed me; I was thirsty and you gave me water; I was a stranger and you invited me into your home; naked and you clothed me; sick and in prison and you visited me. The disciples said, 'Lord, when did we ever see you hungry or thirsty or a stranger or naked or sick or in prison and not help you?' Jesus replied by saying, 'Whatsoever you did to the least of my brethren, you did it to me.' " (Matthew 25:31-46)

"Blessed are the pure of heart: for they shall see God."

Having a pure heart is to act selflessly and spread love freely—not being motivated by self-interest, but being motivated by the common good for God's people. We are to love our neighbors as God loves us. Your heart must not be filled with hatred, anger, and malice; it must be filled with love. The heart is the center of your moral and mental being. A pure heart is the path to feeling the Holy Spirit that lives within each of us.

"Blessed are the peacemakers: for they shall be called children of God."

Are we peacemakers? Peacemakers are those with a spirit of wisdom and mediation. Peacemakers are people who follow after the things which make peace and the things that may edify one another. Instead of adding fuel to a disagreement, they use wisdom and mediation to resolve issues. We should strive to bring peace to the world. War is not the answer, but peace and love are. The more we live in love, the more we are able to spread love, which will ultimately bring peace.

"Blessed are they who are persecuted for righteousness' sake: for theirs is the kingdom of heaven."

Persecuted for righteousness's sake means that a person should not fear the terror or the trouble that may or will come from standing up for God and His people. We should practice spiritual boldness and be ready to stand strong in the face of opposition. Often those who speak and stand up for the common good will be persecuted. Leaders have been assassinated when they chose to stand up for the common good. God is a God of love, and the spirit of fear is not of God.

Traveling to a large metropolitan area in the South, I was struck by the demographic data that was revealed. The city and the state

I visited are plagued with some troubling statistics. The city is one of the poorest metropolitan areas in the United States, has one of the highest crime rates in the state, has one of the highest obesity rates, and in recent years has one of the highest rates of sexually transmitted diseases, including HIV/AIDS, in the country. The state has been a leading state in the payment of minimum wage, but the most dangerous state for violent crimes and meth lab incidents. However, if that was shocking, it was the next statistic that really got my attention—and that is the sheer number of houses of worship existing in this one metropolitan city. The community leaders stated that there are more than 3,000 houses of worship.

Somehow I wanted to reconcile all of this information: the issues that the city and state are confronted with on one hand and, on the other hand, the fact that the area is considered a "Bible Belt" community. I wondered how the community used the Beatitudes that were just described and what those words actually meant to this faith community. I wondered how—and if—these teachings are lived each and every day. I wondered if we are separated by the walls of the religious institutions, versus being united by the Kingdom of God.

This was only one community, but there are many others. I wondered why we feel so powerless to make a difference. One has to wonder. About 10 years ago, I started having this feeling. I guess it was more like a dream, except I was wide awake. Maybe it was a vision. Whatever it was, it would start out the same. I would get this picture in my mind of churchgoers on their way to a worship service. They would arrive at a house of worship, but somehow were not able to enter the building. Meanwhile, in my dream, this same phenomenon is occurring across the nation at the same time. Unable to go inside the buildings, churchgoers begin to have worship services outside. Holding hands and singing, they form a human bridge. From community to community, from state to state, and across the nation, a human bridge is forming. Now that is a new dawn and a "Kingdom" experience!

Humble Beginnings

Growing up in a very rural community in the South, I accepted farming as a way of life. My uncle, a farmer, was never far away from his tractor, a very common sight in the community. Family members and the community were very much a part of working on the farm. It became an experience for the young and the old. There was very little large industry equipment for farming then, and even if there was, during that time small farmers probably would not have had the means to purchase it. Therefore, manual labor on the farm was a common sight and a community event. The smell of tobacco, peanuts, cotton, and corn—not to mention the smell of livestock— filled the air. I did not eat chicken until my senior year in high school, and I am certain it had to do with those years when I stayed with my grandparents and witnessed the manner of death that came for the chickens in the backyard—a "head wrenching" experience. My grandfather showed no mercy.

Although too young to actually work on the farm, it would not have been summer without the younger kids being a part of this experience. The shade trees sheltered the younger ones as the older kids and adults worked in the fields. No matter what other job you had, if you were a family member, you found time to work on the farm; it was a "village" experience. Everyone seemed to know everyone else in the community. Even the teachers knew your family. If you thought that you could get away with something, you remembered quickly that, in a village, all adults were responsible for you, so they would quickly correct you when you did something that you were not supposed to do.

Although neither of my parents went to college, it was never an option for me not to go. It wasn't *whether* you were going, but it was *where*. My father, a World War II veteran, was a man of few words. He was a proud military service member and was a "no-nonsense" kind of person. You knew exactly where you stood with him. His favorite words to me and my brother growing up were, "as long as you live under my roof." In other words, here are the rules of the household, and they are not negotiable. My mother was the only negotiator as far as my father was concerned. Although they ran a tight ship, they taught me and my brother that service was all about action.

Be a Servant to Others (How May I Serve?)

The Christmas season is a season symbolizing the essence of love, the birth of Jesus Christ. Yes, there is the element of hustle and bustle, but there is also something special that happens during Christmas, Kwanzaa, and Hanukkah season: There is an overflowing of love. We seem to think more about giving and find more opportunities to bring joy to someone else's life. Around Thanksgiving a few years ago, I was visiting my family in my hometown in North Carolina. My mom and I decided to go by the nursing home to visit a relative, my mom's nephew (my cousin). Only 60 years old, he was in a nursing home due to a debilitating spinal condition. As we were talking to him, he began to tell us about his son who was hospitalized at a Veteran Affairs Medical Center in Virginia. He said his son was suffering from a disease that sometimes leads to periodic blindness and loss of feeling and sensation in his limbs. I soon learned that the affliction is called Devic's disease, a rare condition that affects eyesight, as well as the spinal cord and nervous system.

That Christmas season, I decided that I was going to be a servant to the family. I knew the mother had been carrying the burden as caretaker and traveling back and forth from North Carolina to be with him. As the story of his condition unfolded, I learned that it was just after the onset of the Iraq War, while serving in the military, that he was stricken with this disease. When I first visited him at the VA, he was 38 years old, six-foot-one inches tall, and 115 pounds. He was bedridden and had no use of his lower body. When I visited him that week, I decided to be of service. Since I have a professional background in healthcare administration, I wanted to help this family improve the quality of life for this young man. I was going to be an advocate for this family and help them navigate the healthcare system, which sometimes can be frustrating. The mother was present on the day I visited. I knew that, based on her comments, she was very concerned about the quality of care he was receiving and didn't feel that she was getting any answers. I knew that, even if this was only her perception, the concern was very real to her. I decided I would need to meet with the administration, or the patient advocate at the facility, to see if I could help resolve some of his mother's concerns.

At this point, he could only move his body from his waist up and he suffered from paralysis from the waist down. My heart ached. I wanted to help a family member, and I had to believe that I would attract all the people I needed to talk to, the people who could truly help me. As I stood at the foot of his bed, his mother was busy tidying his room. I couldn't help but notice his frail body, very weak and seemingly malnourished. He was fed intravenously. He looked up at me with a big smile. I knew that sometimes he would lose his vision, but through his glasses, I could tell that he saw me. He smiled and said, "Come in, cuz. How are you doing? Are you okay?" As I told him I was so glad to see him, I stood there imagining what it must be like for him during the times when he loses his vision, how scared he must be. Fortunately, the loss of vision had always been temporary.

In the middle of our conversation, in walked a middle-aged lady, accompanied by someone else. I soon learned that this was his physician. She said she was making her rounds, checking on him to see how he was doing. She asked him if he wanted any spiritual counseling from one of the chaplains at the facility. I decided to use this opportunity to ask the physician, with my cousin's permission of course, if I could speak to her briefly outside of the room. I looked to my cousin, and he said okay. The physician was extremely nice and very helpful in giving me the whole picture of his care.

I went back into the room. He then received a call from the administrator of the VA nursing home facility where he was being cared for. Once I learned who this individual was, it was my mission to try to meet with her. A couple of hours later, as I walked down the hallway, I randomly stopped someone to ask where I could find the administration offices and told her who I was looking for. The lady looked up at me in amazement and said, "Well, you are looking for me then." Of all the people in the entire facility, I had encountered, in a few hours, the two people—the physician and the administrator—who could be most helpful in my endeavor. They allowed me to attend meetings with the family and the medical team. I do not believe in accidents; it's all about intention. The spiritual energy that each of us has within us allows us to attract the things that are necessary when our intention is aligned with the Source.

My cousin's son passed away the next year, but I feel like I learned a great deal from him during his illness. At his funeral, a letter was read that he wrote. He told the family not to be saddened by his death, but instead to love and love hard. He said not to waste time fighting with one another, but to spend that time, instead, being a blessing to others. These were the words of the pastor when he preached the eulogy: "I knew this young man very well, and I saw his struggles over the years with his illness, but I also saw a young man who was grounded in his faith, and that man was *my* teacher."

It is conceivable to walk in our truth and live our lives knowing that we cannot separate ourselves from one another. Jesus said, "And the King shall answer and say unto them, Verily I say unto you, inasmuch as ye have done it unto one of the least of these my brethren, ye have done it unto me." Matthew 25:40 (KJV) Whether we like it or not, we are connected with one another through one Spirit. No matter what one's religion may be, the common good is the basic premise on which we must agree.

I once had a conversation about brotherly love with a diplomat in Rwanda, Africa. In 1994, nearly one million people were slaughtered in the genocide, while countries—including the United States—did not intervene. Years later, when former US President Bill Clinton was asked about his biggest regret during his administration, he said it was not taking action in Rwanda. A museum in the country is a reminder of the genocide and other genocides that have occurred around the world. As I started talking to this diplomat, I was amazed that our thoughts were so parallel. We lived a world away, yet we were talking about how "we are all connected."

I wondered how things had changed in the country, as years later, the descendants of the same two ethnic groups now live in peace and harmony and try to put the past behind them. Here is where we can learn from our neighbors—remember that our neighbor is next door, across town, in another state, across the country, and yes, even around the globe. An African leader from Uganda, who had been an advisor to the World Health Organization (WHO), once used the term "common good." He said, "We should work for the common good." In spite of our differences, we should work for the common good around the world. It makes sense since we have to share the same planet and breathe the same air. This is not a Democratic or a Republican platform, but it is a principle that could prevent self-destruction.

Our time spent on this earth should be about making the world a better place for the generations to come. When I thought about the younger generations, I wondered if they would see things differently. Would the premise of the common good be more or less attractive to them? This will be examined more closely in Chapter 4 by looking at the millennials.

Clearly, there are those who do not see the benefit of executing humanitarian missions in their backyards—much less around the world. After spending several years working on international projects, I would hear comments such as this: "We need to help our people here in this country [United States]." I think those comments worthy of a response and some additional insights.

We are Americans, living in the home of the free and the land of the brave. Millions of people from all over the world come into our country every year, and millions of Americans travel abroad yearly. We have CDC offices and US embassies in countries all over the world. Those offices work diligently, in tandem with the in-country leaders, to implement programs and to detect, for instance, emerging diseases and disease outbreaks that could become epidemics in the country or even pandemics around the world. US embassies promote US policy interests abroad. Because of the relationships that we continue to build internationally, the United States is much safer. However, there are many other reasons that we benefit from collaborations with foreign countries. Our scientists and professionals have the opportunity to learn through collaborative projects in research. US embassies around the world build relationships with other countries. Humanitarian efforts and infrastructure-capacity building are often seen as powerful ways to decrease the instability in a country—instability that often leads to terrorism. It is certain that whatever happens in another part of the world will sooner or later impact the United States.

California (Embracing Culture
While Working for a Common Goal)

There are no words to describe the experience I had in Northern California. San Francisco/Fremont is considered to be one of the most ethnically diverse areas in our country. The nonprofit consortium organization that I was working with provided healthcare and human services to the neediest in the Tri-City area. Health facilities were scattered throughout the geographic area. The mission was to cross all barriers and all populations. I soon realized the diversity of this community was much like many areas of New York City, with pockets of African Americans, Chinese, Japanese, Hispanic, Vietnamese, and more.

I traveled with the staff and visited many of the communities in order to prepare for a strategic planning workshop that I would conduct at the end of the week. Each community, from Berkeley to Oakland, uniquely showcased its culture. I visited the health facility in the Asian community and the health center in the Hispanic community and many others. Yes, they excitedly shared with me what was unique and special about their communities and their cultures, but that's not where the story ends. It was a reminder to me that we live in a melting pot, filled with rich culture. Many times, such as in the Tri-City area, only a few streets or a short distance separates two groups. You see, what this health consortium realized some time ago is that it is okay for us to celebrate our divergent cultures, but as Americans, we are one and need to work together for *our* country and its peoples' needs. It is that realization and appreciation that makes us come together.

I ended my visit that week with a strategic planning session with representatives from each of these communities. It looked much like a rainbow coalition, an organization fighting for equality and access to healthcare for *all* of its people. You see, they all came together for the common good.

Commitment to Excellence; Share Your Model

The US assistant surgeon general years ago launched a program called Models that Work. The program sought to identify and highlight health programs across the country that could be considered models. A model is generally defined as "the development of a structure or a program that is exceptional, designed to address specific needs within the community and can be replicated." (Webster's definition of "replicate" means to report or copy something exactly.) Many of these programs received federal healthcare funds but used creative approaches and designs to become exceptional.

I was asked to evaluate two such programs considered to be models. One was a homeless program in Baltimore, and the other was a New York City-based health program that was a model for cultural diversity. It was in the late 1990s, and I was in Baltimore working on evaluating the homeless program as part of the Models that Work initiative. This included assessing the model, capturing the essence that made the model unique, and facilitating opportunities to replicate the model nationwide.

The organization in Baltimore used a holistic approach when they cared for the homeless. Most impressive was the networks and links they had built within the community to meet the needs of the population. I met with the leadership and thought I had a good understanding of the model, but I felt that having the opportunity to venture out on the streets would allow for a firsthand look into the eyes of homelessness. I wanted to learn how one program was making a difference.

Two outreach workers were assigned to escort me out into the community. I so admired this young man and young woman, each of whom told his own story of homelessness and incarceration. What better persons to take you on this journey than those who have traveled the same road? I climbed in the car with them, and off we went. First stop was a shelter, then a soup kitchen, transitional housing facility, and substance abuse treatment center. Every place we visited, the passion and the compassion of the staff filled the air. This comprehensive network was woven like a blanket throughout the city, each part designed to meet the needs of the homeless. As the workers in the locations that we visited explained the mission of their organization and their role in treating the homeless, it sounded personal, as if each staff person had found his calling.

My next stop was underneath a bridge by the railroad tracks. The wind howled, and the bitter coldness was a reminder that it was the middle of winter. Going out into the streets was not exactly part of the plan, so I was not dressed for the weather. I wore a long black coat with a hood covered in fur, but I was still freezing. My feet were nearly frozen in my heels. But how could I possibly think about my comfort when, for so many on the streets, this was a way of life? I walked swiftly alongside the outreach workers.

Along the way, they stopped and talked to a young black teen; it appeared that they knew him. He was homeless, and I wanted to know his story. The outreach workers introduced me, and I spoke to him. They asked him if he'd like to tell me his story. He started by saying, "I'm okay, but I couldn't stay there anymore." I was not exactly sure what he meant, but just as I was about to ask him, he looked at me and then looked down at the sidewalk, and said, "I was living with my parents—my mother and stepfather—but things weren't too good." When I asked what he meant, he looked up again. "Well," he said, "my mother was being abused by my stepfather, and I would talk to my mother and tell her she needed to make him stop or get some help." He went on: "My mom would say, 'God is going to take care of it.' I would get so angry at my stepfather. I kept thinking that I was going to kill him, so I decided I was either going to end up in prison for killing someone or on the streets, homeless. Well, I chose the streets."

Somehow I no longer felt the cold; I was transfixed by his words. What a choice, I thought: prison or the streets. Sadly, it's a choice with which too many of our young people are faced. The most recent study by the National Coalition for the Homeless, published in 2008, reported that, based on 2002 data, there were an estimated 1,682,900 homeless and runaway youth.[25]

I finished talking with the young man, and the outreach workers were ready to move on. We walked down a slope to the railroad tracks. On the ground was broken glass and needle syringes—evidence of drug use. I was being careful where I stepped. We were approaching an underpass, so there was some coverage overhead to shelter from the harsh winds and bitter cold. We moved toward an elderly gentleman sitting on a mattress. He seemed to anticipate that we would come over and talk to him, so we headed in his direction. The outreach workers reached in their bags to pull out some snacks that they handed over to the elderly man. He smiled and thanked them. I observed, then moved in closer just as the elderly man started to speak. They had asked him how he was doing, and he said, confidently, "I'm fine." He was sitting on a mattress and motioned to what appeared to be a grocery cart and continued, "I have everything that I need. When I need a shower or clean clothes or food to eat, you see those churches up there?" As he was speaking, I looked to where he was pointing and could see in the distance several churches clustered along the street. He said, "I know where to go, and when to go, to get what I need."

The experience is one that I will never forget. *Meet them where they are. Hear their stories, and then you can really make a difference.* There were many things to observe and learn that day, but the work of these two outreach workers and their personal transformations were now allowing **them** to make a difference in the lives of **others**. Now **that's** a model to replicate.

The Road to Damascus

The Bible speaks about the transformation of a man named Saul, who was one of the most ardent enemies of the early followers of Jesus. Saul is, however, transformed on the road to Damascus when the resurrected Jesus Christ speaks to him. He believes and is later renamed, becoming Paul, an Apostle who wrote 13 of the 27 books in the New Testament of the Bible. God gave Paul the wisdom, strength, and endurance to carry out the mission Jesus had entrusted to him. One of his famous sayings is found in the book of Philippians (4:13): "I can do all things through Christ who strengthens me." I wonder what would have happened if he never had that experience on the road to Damascus, if he had never "heard" the voice of Christ. I think many things in life can cause us to change directions or reevaluate our focus in order to become more purpose driven. Maybe our occurrence is not quite as dramatic as the Road to Damascus story, but each of us has a story.

For some, our change may not be motivated by an instant event, but rather a series of events causing pause. For some, new vision is imparted by the death of a loved one. For others, it may be another occurrence in life. We have seen this happen with politicians. Somehow, purpose on this planet is manifested after a transformative event. To see this concept at work, consider Gabrielle Giffords, the Democratic congresswoman from Arizona who was shot in the head by a mentally disturbed gunman. Her life was spared so she could become an advocate for gun safety. Now the former congresswoman is fighting to ensure that we have common sense gun laws, such as universal background checks.

I also think about what happened in Virginia with Senator Creigh Deeds, who was stabbed multiple times by his son before his son fatally shot himself. Deeds had tried to have his son committed to a mental hospital only days before, but was told there were no available beds. Now, the policy priority for the senator is the fight to ensure that those with mental illness are able to receive the help they need. His life was spared so he could become an advocate for mental health treatment.

And then there is the project I call "Project Guyana." Guyana was a humanitarian assistance contract awarded by the federal government to assess and make recommendations for humanitarian needs in the South American country. But on a personal note, Guyana turned into much more than a contract or a project for me. It was more like a spiritual awakening, a "road to Damascus" experience. It was the releasing of a power that would change my life forever; the experience certainly changed how I see the world.

It was shortly after September 11, 2001, that I was awarded a contract for humanitarian programs that would be launched in South America and the Caribbean. One of the countries involved was the country of Guyana. Most of us will remember Guyana and the Jonestown massacre that occurred at the hands of the religious leader Jim Jones. Reverend Jones left the United States, convincing Americans to leave the country and travel with him to the country of Guyana. He told followers his vision was to build a tropical paradise for them. In 1978, his more than 900 followers lost their lives; some were shot, while others were forced to drink the Kool-Aid-like substance that was laced with cyanide poison. Mothers were forced to kill their babies before killing themselves. Only 33 survivors managed to escape this unspeakable tragedy. Congressman Leo Ryan traveled to Jonestown, Guyana, to seek answers, amidst complaints from the family members back in the United States that persons were being held against their will. However, he was killed in his plane on the gravel airstrip in Jonestown. Mothers, children, and families—seeking love, peace, and freedom—met with their deaths. All of these memories surfaced in my mind as I prepared to take this journey.

In my preparation to fulfill the obligations of the contract, we recruited several teams of subject-matter experts, ranging from physicians, epidemiologists, firefighters, first responders, social workers, HIV/AIDs experts, healthcare administrators, professors, and military experts. I needed to cover the gamut. I had domestic experience in project management, but I did not have any international experience and wanted to make sure that I was surrounded by a team that was knowledgeable and the right fit for this initiative.

Just as important as the experience each would bring to the table was the spirit that the individual could bring to this mission. Often times, "missions" fail—not because of a lack of talent, but because of a lack of passion. We have to be as open to learning as we are to teaching. I wanted to avoid going into a country with even a hint of superiority. I did not want to send the message that "this is the way that you must do this because this is how we do it." So, I was interested in individuals who would assess—and not judge—the country. Rather, we needed those who would try and understand the issues of the health infrastructure, as well as malaria, HIV/AIDS, and emergency preparedness, in order to help the country improve these systems.

I learned from a social worker many years ago that you have to "meet people where they are," and I suppose that applies to communities and a country also. With an average per capita income in the country, at that time, the equivalent of $700 per year, the need was great. The response from consultants was overwhelming; many were interested in this opportunity. But we selected those who would be best for the project. Not everyone had international experience, but that was okay. We selected some without international experience. The next step was to select an administrative director and a medical director. The administrative director for the project would be a dear and trusted colleague and a retired military colonel with over 37 years of military experience in the US Army. The medical director would be a physician who had once served as director for the medical missions carried out by evangelist Pat Robinson. The two of them convened a local summit, a briefing, to meet with the other consultants, look at the task at hand, and understand the state of the country and what challenges we would face.

Last, there would be lots of discussion about cultural competency. The physician had led a team that had performed tens of thousands of medical procedures around the globe. The "airplane-turned-surgery center" would land in a community and the medical team would get to work performing surgeries that would change the lives of so many people. The physician once told me, "The things that we take for granted in the United States are like miracles in many countries, like having a pair of glasses to restore vision."

So everything was set. The colonel and I made advanced trips in order to lay the groundwork for the projects and to discuss meetings and logistics once the team of consultants were in-country. We met several times with the military leadership and the Ministry of Health. The United States had a small military presence, and since the project was sponsored by the US Department of Defense and the US State Department, it was always important to make sure that our plans were in sync with these agencies.

It was a beautiful day in May 2002, and the colonel and I had planned to travel ahead, while the consultants coming into the country would arrive later in the week. The early arrival would allow us to have high-level preliminary meetings and firm up the schedules for the meetings that week for each of the consultant teams. It was early Sunday morning, and I drove to the Richmond airport. With the September 11th tragedy less than a year before, it was very much a part of the American consciousness. I had planned to fly to Atlanta and meet the colonel in Miami, where we would then fly to Guyana.

Once we boarded the plane and the doors closed, the pilot made an announcement that there was a ground hold in Atlanta. No planes were being allowed to land so we had to remain in Richmond. The indication was that this would be a major delay, so I pulled out my cell phone and phoned the colonel. When I told him about the situation, he said, "You have to get off the plane and drive up to DC and take a flight here, otherwise we will not make it to the country today." Emphatically I explained, "The cabin door is closed, and I am sure they will not let me off the plane." He pushed back. Before I knew it, I was out of my seat walking down the aisle to the front of the plane all the while thinking that there were probably post-9/11 air marshals on board who had been trained to respond to any threats. I still cannot figure out why I didn't just press the call button for the flight attendant to come to my seat. Still probably overwhelmed, I explained to the flight attendant that I needed to get off the plane, that I had a very important meeting in Georgetown, Guyana with the US ambassador and the country's leadership the following day, and that if I did not arrive that evening, I would clearly jeopardize the entire mission.

The attendant picked up the phone and made a call to the pilot, stating, "I have a lady here" and she repeated exactly what I had just said. Hanging up the phone, she said, "Follow me." She escorted me off the plane, then she told me, "They will pull your luggage, but you must pick it up at the Delta counter." Little did I realize that was just the first obstacle! I ran to the counter and nearly fell over when I saw a "post 9/11" line. The line was literally stretched out the building. Flying definitely had changed. I just knew I could not stand in that line for hours. I walked outside to the sky captain and asked, "Please, sir, I need you to retrieve my bag from behind the counter. The airline says they have pulled it." He looked at me unapologetically and stated, "I'm sorry, ma'am, but you will have to get in line." Somehow, I kept thinking, *If I just keep moving, God is going to open a door or a window.*

A few minutes went by, and I walked up to another sky captain. "Sir, here is something for you or your kids," I said as I handed him a tip. "I need your help." I thought, *If you don't like the results that you are getting, you have to change your approach.* The sky captain just gave me a long look and then took off. Within two minutes he came out from behind the counter with my luggage. He even asked me where I needed to take it! I stated, "I need a taxi to get to DC." I hopped in the taxi, and we were on the way. The entire time I was talking to the colonel as he was searching to get me on the same flight that he was on. This was risky. What if there were no seats left? Yes it was a gamble, but I had to take that chance. It worked. I was booked to fly out later that evening with a short layover in Barbados.

Due to flight delays, the colonel and I did not arrive in-country until almost midnight—much later than the eight p.m. scheduled arrival time. Normally we would have traveled to the hotel in an armored US vehicle provided by the State Department, but without such transportation, we made the decision to use one of the drivers at the airport. We knew of potential risks, as Americans traveling to many countries are warned against using taxis selected randomly at airports. We had heard that Americans were targets of kidnappings and robberies. So how would we know whom to trust?

Finally, we climbed into a van layered with multicolored carpeting from the roof to the floor. The driver smiled and seemed very kind. Although I was hesitant, my colleague convinced me that it was okay. I was aware, thanks to previous briefings we had with the Guyanese, that civil unrest was taking place in the country between the Afro-Guyanese, of African descent, and the Indo-Guyanese, of Indian descent. Police had been killed, and Americans were advised to take extra precautions.

The hotel was a 45-minute ride from the airport. We had traveled the road before on a previous visit, so I was familiar with the journey. There were virtually no lights on the mostly gravel road, and the darkness was uncomfortable at best. But this time, traveling this long road in a taxi at midnight seemed very different. I started rehearsing in my mind the discussions for the meetings that we would have the next morning to make sure that everything was in place prior to the consultants' arrival later that week. The pressure was on to make sure that this project was successful; after all, we were representing the United States. So, I was rehearsing in my mind as we traveled. I tried to tune out the potholes, the animals dodging across the road, and the darkness of the night.

Next, I remember looking up from the backseat through the front window of the van to find the lights of our vehicle shining upon armed soldiers in front of us with M16 machine guns. The formation appeared to be a roadblock. My heart seemed to stop; I could no longer hear my breath. I turned to my colleague in silence, hoping that his expression would give me some assurance that this was routine and that we were okay, but he did not seem sure. The van suddenly came to a complete stop as one of the soldiers slowly walked over to the van. He appeared to be in a military uniform, and he motioned for the driver to open the door of the vehicle. The driver slowly complied.

My body felt numb, perhaps from my shallow breathing; it were as if my body was too afraid to take deep breaths. I thought they were going to ask us to step out, and I was paralyzed with fear for our safety. Knowing the civil unrest taking place in the country, I had to wonder if we were being targeted. I did not know why we were being stopped. I had only read about or seen news reports about military coups that overthrow a government. My thoughts moved faster than lightning. As the driver slowly opened the door, the soldier looked inside the van. While I'm sure this took only a few seconds, it seemed like hours. Never completely stepping in, he looked toward the back of the van, where we were sitting. I only briefly made eye contact. He then closed the door and waved for our driver to continue. The driver did so, and I started breathing again.

I believe that when things happen in our lives, it gives us the opportunity to ask ourselves the very important questions: Who are we? Why are we here on this earth? And are we living on purpose? Dr. Wayne W. Dyer, a renowned spiritual leader, produced a movie called *The Shift.*[26] I saw the movie years after my Guyana experience; the movie helped to explain something that happens during an internal shift in our lives. What we experience is called a quantum moment, and it usually follows a low point or an event in our lives.

We made it to the hotel, but the colonel and I never even spoke about what happened. That next morning, we were off to the US Embassy for some scheduled meetings. It was the last opportunity to finalize the plans before beginning the formal assessments we were about to conduct. The meeting was with the senior military leaders of Guyana to review the plans for the remainder of the week. We spoke about several humanitarian projects planned, and we agreed on the most-needed areas, like the health infrastructure; vector-borne diseases, such as malaria caused by mosquitos; firefighting and first responder capability in the country; and other necessary humanitarian operations.

But there was one area discussed that seemed to strike a nerve, and that was HIV/AIDS treatment. You see, this was prior to the launch of President George W. Bush's Emergency Plan for AIDS Relief (PEPFAR) program. Medications and treatment for AIDS did not exist outside the United States, and many were dying from the disease. The intent of this project was to assess the current status of the disease in Guyana, which would include the development of a long-term plan for treatment.

Well, this was not an easy task because, at the time, many saw AIDS as the curse brought to people by God for their sinful nature. As I merely brought up the plan to conduct the HIV/AIDS assessment, one leader—who was the spokesperson for the group—a young, female epidemiologist in the military, responded. Her words rebuffed even the mention of the HIV/AIDS assessment: "I'm not sure you understand. . . . We are a religious nation." I could see that I had insulted her. She went on by saying, "There are those who believe that if people have this disease, then it's a punishment from God." I was in shock. I remember leaning back in my chair thinking, *What have I done? Should I just let this go? Maybe we will conduct all the other projects, but this one, I should not pursue.*

But flashing before my eyes were the masses of people with AIDS being thrown in hospice houses left to die, as was the practice. This atrocity, to me, was being done in the name of religion. I thought about the experience of being stopped on that lonely, dark road the night before. Maybe my presence before this Guyanan leader was somehow part of God's plan. I asked myself, *What has your life truly meant on this earth? In the most difficult of times, can you stand in your truth?*

I knew what I had to do. This wasn't just about a project. I was being called, in that moment, to stand in my truth and speak for God's people. After my words, which I am sure did not come from me but were birthed from the Divine out of love, there was a quiet calm that filled the room. The meeting ended shortly afterward, and I thought, *Well, Juanita, you just blew that, and you've jeopardized this entire mission.* I even thought we might receive a call from the US government, saying we were to return home because we had just pissed off this foreign country's leaders.

Nevertheless, we continued to make plans, picking up the team of consultants that evening at the airport and preparing for the kickoff meeting. The next morning, we held our entrance meeting with community leaders, US government agencies that were in-country, and the consultants we had selected for the assessments.

Just before the meeting started, in walked the young Guyanan woman with whom I had the conversation about AIDS treatment. She was accompanied by her team. She walked through the crowded room and straight over to me. *Well, here it goes*, I thought. She then embraced me, with a hug and a kiss on the cheek. I nearly fell to the floor. That was my confirmation that she would take care of everything to make sure that we could continue with all the projects at hand. Maybe something had happened in the room the day before. I know now that one heart can speak to another heart, and touching just one heart can create a domino effect. If we can remove the ego and speak directly from one heart to another heart, then we can make a difference in the world—one heart at a time.

As for the team of professionals, I've talked to most of them over the years, and it is not difficult to see how this experience changed their lives. The team of firefighters and first responders from the Dallas, Texas, firefighting academy introduced an initiative for the city of Dallas to provide used firefighting apparatus to the country of Guyana, after they observed this was desperately needed while in-country. The firefighters had witnessed an actual fire in one community, and we watched as it burned through the community. These experienced professionals, who had trained many students, could only stand by and watch helplessly as the fire spread through the block, burning the old wooden buildings like paper. Businesses and homes went up in flames. The locals were running with buckets of water from the river to help put out the fire. The water pressure from the hoses of the very old fire trucks seemed more like water squirting from a toy water gun than a fire hose. There were no helmets or gloves for protection. I am sure that witnessing this devastation firsthand was the force that drove these team members to take action once they returned to the States. They were in the right place at just the right time. There are no accidents.

An associate professor at a school of public health in Virginia, who did the medical-vector assessment for malaria, described how he has since used his experience in Guyana in his teachings at the university. Others said they made major personal decisions in their lives after returning. One gay member on the team reconnected with his friend of many years, and they ended up getting married. The US government, under PEPFAR, introduced the treatment of HIV/AIDS to America in 2003, one year later, but I knew that we opened that door in another nation by speaking to and reaching one heart. The right person was in the right place at the right time.

CHAPTER 3

Ordinary People, Extraordinary Triumph

Lord, make me an instrument of thy peace.
Where there is hatred, let me sow love;
Where there is injury, pardon;
Where there is doubt, faith;
Where there is despair, hope;
Where there is darkness, light;
Where there is sadness, joy.
O divine Master, grant that I may not so much seek
To be consoled as to console,

To be understood as to understand,
To be loved as to love;
For it is in giving that we receive;
It is in pardoning that we are pardoned;
It is in dying to self that we are born to eternal life.
—Saint Francis of Assisi

Change begins with each of us. One person can change the heart of a country—and the world. That is the story of Dr. King, Gandhi, and Nelson Mandela. It happened in America, in India, and in South Africa. A movement occurred. There was a shift in the consciousness of a people. At this moment a shift—a transformation—is needed in our country, but it has to start within each of us. Changes are occurring each and every day. DNA is now being used to free innocent prisoners from the death penalty. It's hard to imagine a country in the industrialized world where an innocent person can be wrongly sentenced and put to death. The Internet now makes it possible to connect to someone across the world in an instant. We are more *connected* than ever, and the opportunities to help have never been greater. However, we see things differently based on whether we are looking at them through the Spirit or from our limited five senses, which are associated with our egos. The ego can quickly reduce a world of opportunities to a mere story on the evening news. Never lose sight of the bigger picture and the new awareness emerging inside of you.

You become what you think about all day, and those days become your lifetime.
—Dr. Wayne W. Dyer

The Journey

When you are passionate about something, you will find a way, through your intention, to move into that calling. I've met many people on *my* journey, and I realize that they are also on *their* journey. Many became my inspiration for writing this book.

God is love, and His love is unconditional. I believe, in our journey in this life, we are to love others the same way: unconditionally. There is no challenge in loving your friends, but try loving those who are not very friendly. That kind of love may require a change on our part. Nevertheless, we cannot expect change without first looking in the mirror. Yes, change must begin within each of us. No one could have said it better than Michael Jackson in the song "Man in the Mirror." I was familiar with the tune, but when I actually listened to what was being said, I realize how true the words are.

Wonderful people all over the county have looked in that mirror and have made that change. We can all become what we want to see in others.

A War Hero

It was late morning one spring. I gathered in the offices of a law firm with several other businessmen and women to discuss collaborating on a few government projects. Some were sitting around the table, and some were standing along the sides of the wall in the room. I only knew a few of the people there. We took turns introducing ourselves. There were men, women, African Americans, Caucasians, and Native Americans present. The man sitting beside me was very quiet. He was African American and had a small build; he said his name was Fred Cherry. I did not know the name, and he did not say much else. Since I did not know the name nor the person, I did not think too much of his short introduction. However, there were some in the group that day who knew Fred, and they asked him if he would share his story. So I looked to my right as he began to speak. In a few short minutes, I learned that I was sitting next to a war hero, but not just any war hero, a POW (prisoner of war).

You see, Fred was a fighter pilot in the US Air Force during the Vietnam War when his plane was shot down in October 1965. He was the first and the highest-ranking black officer captured by the North Vietnamese and was held longer than any black man ever held in captivity in Vietnam. He would spend over seven and a half years as a prisoner of war, until his release in February 1973. He survived the torture, the horrible conditions, and for the most part, the isolation. He never broke the code or gave up US secrets.

Back in the United States during that time, we were in the throes of the Civil Rights Movement. The Vietnamese felt that because of the persecution and brutality that blacks were subjected to in the U S, no black from the U S would care enough for the country to protect *any* military secrets. Fred remembers when they broke the news to him in 1968 that Dr. Martin Luther King had been assassinated. It was devastating, and he fought back the tears. He remained loyal and committed to his country. I can imagine the Vietnamese must have been in disbelief. No matter what they tried, they could not break his spirit.

Getting to know Fred over the years has been such a humbling experience and has certainly impacted my own life in many ways. What is so amazing is how any human being could go through the types and frequency of torture that this man went through and not harbor anger and bitterness. In later years, he went back to Vietnam to make peace and forgive his captors, and this was portrayed in a documentary. Speaking to youth and to military service members around the country, he has told his story many times. Fred's survival for those seven and a half years teaches us something that we cannot ignore: Our strength is not our physical bodies, it is instead our soul and our spirit.

In the day when I cried, you answered me and strengthened me with strength in my soul.

—Psalm 138:3

It Just Wasn't My Time; I Still Had Work to Do

I was sitting and talking to a miracle. Statistically, no one survives a brain aneurism without getting medical care within a matter of hours, but Susan did. And her care was delayed not just hours, but for days. Susan is a foot solider, a program coordinator for a federally funded healthcare program in North Carolina; her patients love her. I had met Susan years before and had come to know her, but when I saw her again, there was something quite different. Middle-aged, with blond hair and a small physique, her head appeared to have been shaved on one side. I initially thought that maybe she now had cancer, a brain tumor of some sort, but I wasn't sure. Then I overheard her telling her story.

Her experience started with just a simple headache one morning; however, being in the healthcare field made her reluctant to rush to the doctor right away. *Maybe I will just take some medication*, she told herself. But the headache worsened, so she knew she had to see a doctor. She went to the doctor, and he gave her some medicine for the headache and sent her home. But the headache did not go away. The pain was severe, so she went back to the doctor again. He changed the medication and sent her home again.

Unbeknownst to her, she was having a brain aneurism, meaning the blood vessels in her brain had ruptured, and her head was bleeding internally. Normally, you have only hours to get medical attention in order to live, yet Susan survived for days while her brain was bleeding. The third time she sought medical attention, she was rushed into surgery, maybe with only minutes left to live after surviving for days in this state. She survived, and every day is a reminder of just how precious life is. But if you think after such a terrifying event she has slowed down, then you are wrong. Instead, each and every day is spent making a difference in the lives of many at the clinic where she works in North Carolina.

It Isn't about Me; It Is about How Many of My "Sisters" I Can Reach

Nothing could have hit closer to home than when one of my closest cousins was diagnosed with breast cancer. At age 40, having spent most of her years as a registered nurse taking care of others, she was about to experience what she could never have imagined. Through the surgery, radiation treatment, and chemotherapy, she did not see herself as just a cancer patient. Right after surgery, she woke up and told her mom, "I know that I have to help other women."

So even during her treatment, she found herself sitting down with a coworker, having lunch and thinking about what they could do to reach other women, especially African-American women, to educate them about breast cancer. African-American women are more likely to die from the disease than Caucasian women. She started an organization in the Raleigh-Durham area called Sisters Triangle

Network. Fifteen years in remission from the cancer, her faith and the work of the nonprofit has reached over 200,000 women, educating them about the disease. The foundation helps patients with money for transportation to see the doctor and with the cost of medication for some. But it didn't stop there. The medical community took notice of her work and her success in reaching women of color, and a few years later Duke Medical Center asked her to lead their cancer outreach program. Through the most difficult circumstances in life can come the greatest blessings, and your greatest gift to mankind may emerge from your most severe struggle.

I Was Saving Their Lives, but They Were Changing Mine

I met a remarkable physician once in rural Alabama. I had traveled to a major city in Alabama, and during my time there, I heard about a doctor who was practicing in a very rural community about three hours outside the major city. I remember a feeling in my heart that I had to meet this doctor. Although I had limited time, I had to find a way to make it happen. That was it; I had made up my mind that I would go, and off I went, accompanied by a colleague.

At first we could not find his medical practice using the directions we had been given. There were no restaurants, and in the rural community, there were few directional signs. There was not even a grocery store in sight. We saw a gas station that looked also like the neighborhood restaurant. I then turned down a gravel road and drove a ways in a wooded area, per the instructions. I remembered that I was supposed to go through a wooded area, and then I would see an opening, and off to the side would be the medical office. I looked to my right, and there it was: a single-wide mobile home gently leaning to the side. Outside the mobile home was a much-used car with the license plates "Omega Psi Phi," a college fraternity that I recognized. I was confident we had arrived at the correct location.

I walked up the ramp and opened the door to see a very crowded waiting room. Glancing down the hallway, I caught a glimmer of a man in a white coat, dodging in and out of the rooms. We introduced ourselves to the staff, and they promptly ushered us to the doctor's office at the end of the hallway. Twenty minutes passed as we waited. I wanted to hear his story. I looked around the office, noticing the pictures and diplomas. He finally walked into the office and apologized for keeping us waiting. I responded with, "No problem," and thanked him for taking the time from his busy schedule to speak with us.

As the conversation unfolded, it was not difficult to see his passion for his work and for his patients. I could not help but think that this well-credentialed physician had left a very successful career in New York City. I was almost certain he could be practicing medicine anywhere else in the country, making a lot more money, but he wasn't; he was here. The community was layered with generational poverty; there were very few resources, but so much need. *What had made him stay?* I wondered. Before I knew it, the question just came out. He leaned forward and looked at me and told me that his wife was from the area and needed to return home to care for a parent. He returned with this wife, and he started practicing medicine in the community. The patients were now like family, he said. Knowing the difficulty of attracting medical providers to the community, he simply did not have the heart to leave, even 18 years later. He was living on purpose.

What person could better understand the needs of a community than someone providing services in that community? When asked his thoughts about what resources would make his life easier, he paused for a moment then said, "Resources for patient education." I was expecting his request to be much larger, considering the need, but it was so simple. St. Francis of Assisi's words came to mind: "Preach the Gospel at all times, and when necessary, use words." This rural doctor's life was the sermon. He was saving their lives, but they were changing his.

The St. Francis quote gives me pause in that people will know you by your deeds, the life you live. A friend of mine, a reverend, once told me, "You really don't look down on people, do you? The only time you look down is to pick someone up." I really had not thought about it much in that way, because many of the people I've met on my spiritual journey are truly the inspiration for me. Regardless of which side of the tracks we come from, we still come from the same Source. Whether we are trying to find our way or whether we are making a way for others, somehow I know we are all connected.

"Without love, there is no reason to know anyone, for love will in the end connect us to our neighbors, our children and our hearts"

—Dr. Martin Luther King, Jr.

Practice What You Preach

I was in one of the Southern states: South Carolina. I met a physician who pulled me aside during a meeting and asked me a question that would leave me without words. Although I will probably never see him again, I will never forget what he said. The mission of the health center I was touring was to serve an underserved population, predominately African Americans. As I toured the facility, the physician politely pulled me aside and asked me, "Can I speak to you for a moment—if you don't mind?" I excused myself from the rest of the group and entered his office. He looked at me and sort of stared, which was making me a little self-conscious. He then said, "You know, you seem to me to be an open-minded person." (Maybe he was judging me from my line of questions on the tour; other than that, I wasn't quite sure how he would know.) He continued, "So I was wondering if I might ask you a question." He went on to say, "Not long ago, civil rights leaders descended upon the capital here in protest of the Confederate flag that hung on the steps of the capital." I remembered what he was talking about because it certainly had made the news. Then he said, "Some held such anger for what many others felt was a display of pride and heritage. But my question is this: Why do you think African Americans aren't as outraged about how HIV/AIDS is affecting the African-American community—especially here in the South? Why isn't there just as much anger over how this disease is devastating the community?"

I was stunned by this question, coming from a white physician; I certainly wasn't expecting it. I was immediately conflicted. I could feel a battle going on inside of me. It was a battle that made me want to defend the actions and outrage caused by the display of the Confederate flag. I mean, what right did he have to ask me the question in the first place? How could he possibly understand the pain caused by that part of our country's history?

But remember, I said there was a battle that was going on inside of me as I struggled with the question. *Battle* means that there was an opposing side. I understood the struggle, and I had to admit to myself that I did not understand why the African-American community has been so silent as this disease has increasingly affected the African-American community at a disproportionate rate, especially impacting our youth. I think somehow he must have been aware of the battle as I struggled to resolve this issue in my own mind in order to answer the question. I was simply trying to find the right words. My ego was saying one thing, and my heart was saying something different. Though it seemed like a lifetime had gone by, it was no more than a few seconds.

As I opened my mouth, still not sure of what was coming out, he continued. I politely allowed him to keep talking, thinking maybe there was more to this story. He said that a few years ago, he was in private medical practice and most of the patients he saw were covered by some form of medical insurance. He said he was in the prime of his career, but he started noticing more and more patients showing up at his offices with no medical insurance—not to mention that many of them were HIV infected, and most were African American. He said, "No doctor wanted to see them, and I became so frustrated. I knew I had to do something because, without treatment, they would die. I made a big decision to start seeing these patients, knowing that there would be no insurance to bill. What else was I supposed to do? It significantly impacted my income. I even sold off some of my assets to offset the expenses." I somehow knew that this was so much bigger than the question itself. It was really about how we, as a society, have become desensitized to the pain and suffering of mankind, even the death of those around us.

As a point of reference it should be noted that according to the CDC, blacks/African Americans continue to experience the most severe burden of HIV, compared with other races and ethnicities. Blacks represent approximately 12 percent of the US population, but accounted for an estimated 44 percent of new HIV infections in 2010. They also accounted for 44 percent of people living with HIV infection in 2009. Since the epidemic began, more than 265,812 blacks with an AIDS diagnosis have died, including an estimated 6,630 in 2011. Unless the course of the epidemic changes, at some point in their lifetime, an estimated one in 16 black men and one in 32 black women will be diagnosed with HIV infection.[27]

The sacrifice of this doctor, just one human being, should not have surprised me, but it did. How quick we are to judge and condemn others. Let's hear their stories; they each have a story. I just stared at him as he spoke, and finally, when I opened my mouth, there was nothing else I could say but "Thank you." Really, there were no words left, for this physician embodied something that was so profound. It was as if he had just reached in and grabbed my heart. And well, his question about the flag was truly a sincere question, from a man who had given so much.

My Pain Has Been Used as a Blessing for Others

He was soft-spoken and worked in the field of social work. I am always curious as to how people end up in various careers. Many times, the careers we train for and start out in will not be where we end up. Our journey moves us closer to our true purpose. It's like the gravitational pull of the purpose is somewhat natural. It even feels natural.

I had seen this particular man on the highway one day, and about a week later, I bumped into him in the grocery store. That caught my attention. Here was someone I did not know and had never seen before, but all of a sudden, I had seen him twice in one week. Well, since I do not believe in coincidence, I had to believe there was some reason he had suddenly appeared in my life. He worked for the county, and I thought maybe he could be a business contact; maybe we'd keep in touch. We exchanged business cards and went on our way.

A few weeks later, we made contact, and over time, I learned his story. I am always interested in how people end up where they are. His career as a social worker is purely about helping others escape from their situations and getting their lives back on track. His story is full of pain, but he had learned to use the pain in his own life for the good of others. Growing up without a mother, his siblings were placed with different family members. He remembers vividly the exact moment at 13 years old when he heard that his mother had passed. He was the oldest of eight siblings. He went with his youngest sibling to live with his great grandparents, and the remaining siblings were placed with other family members. He found sports to be his outlet for the pain during that time, lettering in four sports in high school. But after sports and college, he needed more. After trying out a number of different jobs, he finally ended up in the field of social work, with a focus on the youth, especially youth from troubled homes. He would have to use the experience of his own personal journey to effect change in the lives of others.

One of his greatest moments was not just receiving an award from the county for a youth program that he had started in the community, but it was receiving an invitation to the graduation of one of the youth who had been in his program—from Harvard University. He told me, "Maybe I had a small role in that student's journey and her career path." He still thinks about his mom, but uses the energy of those moments for good. He wrote this poem as if he hears the voice of his mother speaking to him. It is very moving.

I Am Poem

I am . . . Martha Mason.

I wonder . . . why we parted.

I hear . . . your voice each day.

I see . . . that you are touching the lives of many people.

I want . . . to always be remembered.

I am . . . your mother.

I pretend . . . not to hurt.

I feel . . . empty.

I touch . . . your face when you think it's the wind.

I worry . . . when you don't take time for yourself.

I cry . . . sometimes out of joy that God has given you direction.

I am . . . your mother.

I understand . . . your journey has been rough.

I say . . . continue to trust God.

I dream . . . that we will be together again.

I try . . . to not dwell on what your earthly issues are.

I hope . . . our destination brings us to one common place.

I am . . . your mother.

CHAPTER 4

The Millennials: A Chosen Generation

But you are not like that, for you are a chosen people. You are royal priests, a holy nation, God's very own possession. As a result, you can show others the goodness of God, for he called you out of the darkness into his wonderful light.

—1 Peter 2:9

One might wonder if Peter, in the passage above, was talking about the millennials when he said, "You are a chosen people. As a result, you can show others the goodness of God, for he called you out of the darkness into his wonderful light." The characteristics of the generations and what they stood for and still stand for is fascinating. Looking back over the last 100 years, there have been five generations that have been named, based on different characteristics. The Greatest Generation was born between 1900 and 1924 and was the generation that fought and won World War II. My dad was born in this generation and was a World War II veteran. The Silent Generation, born 1925–1945, was born in the middle of the Great Depression and during World War II. My mom was born during this generation. Considered silent compared to the noisy Baby Boom Generation, they did not exactly "stir things up;" they were mostly considered conformists.

The baby boomers were born between 1946 and 1964, when childbirths dramatically increased after the end of World War II. Yes, I am a "boomer." Boomers have a very high work ethic; some have been considered workaholics. If your work ethic is not up to par with a boomer, he might even consider you lazy. Generation X, born 1965–1979, are considered savvy and entrepreneurial loners. X's identify themselves as technologically savvy. Now as for the millennials, born from 1980 to 2000, they consider themselves to be more socially liberal , fiscally conservative and tolerant.

Could the Millennials be the "chosen generation"? Will the millennials be the generation committed to the common good? Just who are the millennials, and why do their opinions matter so much? Seems like everyone is trying to figure them out. Many talk about the millennials as being the future of our country. As most of the millennials are coming of age, they are starting to move into the political scene. Take note of the movements associated with this generation: the Dreamers, for immigration reform; the Dream

Defenders, who desire to develop the next generation of leaders to disrupt the structures that oppress our communities; the Black Youth Project, based on three concepts: knowledge, voice, and action. All of these movements have a common theme about empowerment and disrupting the status quo. This is about our youth taking a stand.

So just who are the millennials? There are over 80 million of these young adults in the United States. They are considered to be the largest generation in American history. They are the children of the baby boomers. According to David D. Burstein, "[Millennials] are fast becoming the most influential demographic slice of the American pie, disproportionately driving economic indicators and social, cultural, and political trends. In many countries in Africa, the Middle East, and Asia, Millennials make up over a third or even half the population. World-wide, there are 1.7 billion Millennials—almost one-third of the people on earth." [28] It has been said that this generation is more focused on the common values of society. So what better place to profile this generation than in a book about the common good? In many ways, they mirror their elders with strong family values; in other ways, they are the opposite of the baby boomers—not exactly workaholics, you might say. When I grew up, you were taught by your parents: Get an education so you can get a good job; work hard and you will do well. I guess that's how their generation defined success.

Millennials are very educated, but tend not to be overly religious as you would find in the elder generation. Nevertheless, they are spiritual. A Pew Research poll shows only one in four affiliated with any particular faith. Yet in other ways, millennials remain fairly traditional in their religious beliefs and practices . . . for instance, young adults' beliefs about life after death and the existence of heaven, hell and miracles closely resemble the beliefs of older people today. Millennials are no less convinced than their elders that there are absolute standards of right and wrong. And they are slightly more supportive than their elders of government efforts to protect morality, as well as somewhat more comfortable with involvement in politics by churches and other houses of worship. They are very family oriented but are not rushing to get married. However, millennials are on track to become the most educated generation in American history and have been enrolling in graduate school in record numbers because of the lack of jobs and the lagging economy. They are history's first "always connected" generation, steeped in digital technology and social media.[29]

There are probably many things that have influenced how this group behaves. After all, most lived through 9/11; they've experienced the Gulf War and grew up during the Iraq and Afghanistan wars. They turned out to the polls in massive numbers to elect the first African-American US president. However, mass murders, such as at Virginia Tech, Fort Hood, Tucson, the Aurora, Colorado theater, and Sandy Hook have become all too familiar. They've witnessed bombings, like in Oklahoma City and at the Boston Marathon. The natural disasters, such as Hurricane Katrina and Hurricane Sandy, made them more interested in issues related to climate change. In the case of Katrina, they may have had a firsthand look at the face of racism and poverty and the vulnerabilities of certain populations as they and others around the country watched in horror as people stood helplessly on the rooftops of houses and other buildings for days with signs pleading for help. They watched as the predominately African-American crowd at the Super Dome endured the smothering heat of New Orleans, waiting days for help from the government and watching loved ones wither away and die from the extreme conditions. Millennials have also lived through the financial crisis and the lingering effects of the crisis as it made job opportunities more difficult to come by. These are just a few of the things that may influence their outlook on the world and shape their concerns about what is happening around the world.

Certainly 9/11 had an impact on our country and affected every American. The most horrific act that one could imagine ultimately brought Americans closer together. People sought religion for comfort, flocked to churches, expressed random acts of kindness, and were more sympathetic and tolerant in the aftermath. Enlistment in the military escalated and patriotism grew. Everyone was looking for a way to demonstrate their "love of country." Individuals became more interested in international affairs and the happenings around the world. It became more and more difficult for Americans to "tune out" what was happening globally. Global issues and the desire to find solutions to the world's problems began to rise to the consciousness of the millennials. On several international trips that I've taken, I've been amazed to see so many high school students on their way to a developing country; they go to teach, to serve, and to be a part of the solution.

Millennials have played a major role in politics, even turning out in mass numbers to the voting polls in 2008 to help elect the first African-American president. They embraced the "change" that President Barack Obama ran on. They are certainly not afraid to embrace diversity and equality. Yes, most millennials support same-sex marriage and have actively participated in lesbian, gay, bisexual, and transgender (LGBT) movements. Millennials do not necessary have "brand" loyalty, but they tend to look for companies that are "socially conscious." Social entrepreneurship is very attractive to a millennial. Their focus is on making the world a better place. They are well versed in technology, have strongly embraced the digital world, and seem to be leaders in the innovations that occur in social media. Millennials are the only generation that doesn't cite "work ethic" as a top priority. However, they tend to be the most optimistic about the future of the nation. Sounds confusing, right? They are not overly concerned about work ethic, but they are optimistic about the future of the nation.

I met Soundarya in 2011 as I was returning from a trip to Tanzania, Africa. Soundarya is from India. We both had a connecting flight from Europe, and she ended up sitting beside me on the flight to the United States. I was extremely exhausted from my work and the travel, so all I wanted to do was sleep. She seemed edgy and just kept turning around in the seat. The fidgeting seemed more like nervous energy. I thought that maybe she was just nervous about flying, or maybe it was her first trip to the United States and she was excited. I soon turned away, closing my eyes, hoping that I could get a little shuteye and somehow tune out what was going on next to me. It did not work. With my back to her, she continued to toss and turn in the chair. I soon realized that I could not ignore her. She had my attention—if that is what she wanted—and so she got it.

I sat up in my chair, looked over at her, and struck up a conversation. I soon learned that it was, indeed, her first trip to the United States, and she was so excited that she found it hard to sit still. She had been selected as one of 30 young girls around the world to receive a scholarship to attend an internship in Washington state.

Soundarya was only one of two selected from India to participate. So, she did have reason to be excited—what an honor. The purpose of the program was to focus on the status of women and the empowerment of young women around the world.

She was only 20 years old, but in so many ways, her sense of purpose and her passion seemed far beyond her years. She is a millennial. She spoke of her faith and a "knowing" that she would achieve her dreams. Little by little, she started to unveil her story. She grew up in a small village that, by India's standards, would be considered middle class. Children's rights are not respected in all countries, and in many countries children are exploited. This treatment can sometimes include depriving them of education and forcing them into child labor. Young girls often are forced into marriage. After high school, she had to go to work to support her family and to support continuing her education. She spoke of her ailing parents and grandparents all living under one roof. She worked to put herself through college, performing with excellence so that she could get as many scholarships as possible. (According to a World Health Organization article published in March 2013, "14.2 million girls marry annually or 39,000 daily who will marry too young. Between 2011 and 2020 more than 140 million girls will become child brides, according to United Nations Population Fund (UNFPA). Furthermore of the 140 million girls who will marry before they are 18, 50 million will be under the age of 15. In South Asia, nearly half of young women and in sub-Saharan Africa more than one third of young women are married by their 18th birthday. In terms of absolute numbers, because of the size of its population, India has the most child marriages . . . in 47% of all marriages the bride is a child . . . Dr. Osotimehin, Executive

Director UNFPA states child marriage is an appalling violation of human rights and robs girls of their education, health and long-term prospects.")[30]

Income for Soundarya and her family sometimes only covered the rent for housing in the village and her school fees. At times, food and medicines were not options. I felt the pain in her voice as she spoke about the difficulties, but I also sensed in this conversation a strong spiritual tone, where her desire to help women in her country was manifested. She told me, "Education is the key to improving the economics that prevent women from participating fully in society." Did I mention that we had this conversation when she was only 20 years old? She said, "Everything that is happening is part of God's plan to fulfill my purpose here on earth." Just finishing her master's in economics, she believed she was on the right track. I interviewed her because I was interested in her opinions in a number of areas.

Me: How has your experience growing up in India defined who you are?

Soundarya: "Defeat the defeat before the defeat defeats you." This is the line which defines me as a person. Growing up, I didn't have many positive role models after whom I would want to pattern my life. My family's financial situation forced me to work once I finished high school. Thank good fortune that I got a job with a reasonable salary to have our daily bread. I have never lamented to God for giving me those hitches at a very young age; rather, I thank the Almighty for enriching me with powerful experiences in life. Observing the daily struggles that I encountered, I sought a different path in life. By doing this, I set goals for myself, made wise choices that would yield rewards instead of consequences, and surrounded myself with positive individuals who could provide me with the guidance needed to achieve my goals. I often found myself reevaluating and assessing my objectives in order to remain focused and to make sure that my goals aligned with my dreams and aspirations in life.

Me: Your vision is to make the world a better place for women. Are you up for the challenge?

Soundarya: Challenges are what make life interesting, and overcoming them is what makes life meaningful. Yes, now I can challenge and defeat any tough situation. As a woman, I've always visualized becoming an ethical, smart, and diplomatic leader. I consistently had a passion for economic development and leadership, which was the reason to take a graduate course in economics.

Me: You mentioned that sports were an important part of your life.

Soundarya: My involvement in sports is an important chapter in my life, as it taught me to be disciplined, to be a leader, and to respect others' talents. It taught me the "killer instinct" and gave me a "fight till your last breath" attitude. I was a volleyball player for seven years, from sixth grade until my higher secondary.

Me: There are a lot of places in the world you could go to pursue your dream. Why the United States?

Soundarya: I would like to come to the United States to study and work. It is the best place in the world to learn new things, with practical knowledge and global exposure.

Truly, it will be a life-changing experience and will help me to develop the required analytical skills to achieve my goal. The flexibility, infrastructure, recognition, and employee support are the best I've come across. The United States of America is the perfect place to gain the needed technological and professional skills and to grow personally so that I may realize my childhood dream of becoming a change-maker.

Me: What role does your faith play in your life?

Soundarya: It's hard to wait around for something you know might never happen, but it's hard to give up when you know it's everything you want.

I have made a commitment to define myself in life through a deep connection with God. Gandhi once said, "What is faith worth if it is not translated into action?"

The differences within the generations and the strategic marketing by companies to target various segments of our population are apparent. But millennials will have a very large role to play in the future of our country. With the gridlock in the US Congress, it is doubtful that we will see major legislative changes unless there is a movement by the people and for the people.

Conversing with millennials by e-mail may be increasingly difficult as they much prefer social media or instant messaging. The good news is that millennials are entrepreneurs. Marvin Cetron and Owen Davies say, "Entrepreneurialism will be a global trend, as members of Generation X and the Millennials throughout the world tend to share values. Gen X and Millennial entrepreneurs are largely responsible for the economic growth in India and China . . . In India, the younger generations dress and think more like their American counterparts than their parents." [31]

I think we are only in the beginning stages of the millennial movement. With the passion motivating the Soundaryas of the world, nothing can stand in the way.

CHAPTER 5

Social Entrepreneurship: The Solution

"Do not worry in the least about yourself, leave all worry to God,"—this appears to be the commandment in all religions. This need not frighten anyone. He who devotes himself to service with a clear conscience, will day by day grasp the necessity for it in greater measure, and will continually grow richer in faith. The path of service can hardly be trodden by one who is not prepared to renounce self-interest, and to recognize the conditions of his birth. Consciously or unconsciously, every one of us does render some service or other. If we cultivate the habit of doing

this service deliberately, our desire for service will steadily grow stronger, and will make not only for our own happiness but that of the world at large.

—Gandhi

Entrepreneurship is probably one of the areas that unites those on the right and the left in politics. Everyone equally seems to support the idea of entrepreneurship and free enterprise. But there is an emerging concept and business practice that is gaining attention and traction in the business community, and that is *social* entrepreneurship. We can make a significant difference in the world through social entrepreneurship.

Not a new concept, social entrepreneurship generally seeks innovative solutions to society's problems. These businesses and organizations are driven to create or add value to society. They measure success by the impact the business has on society, while at the same time creating an entity that is sustainable and profitable. The innovation of these companies can make life easier and healthier and the environment friendlier. Even businesses that have not committed their entire enterprise to social entrepreneurship have committed a portion of profit for causes that benefit communities. When the economy is struggling, social entrepreneurship can be invaluable. These businesses can be for profit or not for profit. They can strengthen local communities by hiring local people, especially in areas with high unemployment. In order to have a successful company, the motivation cannot be revenue alone. There must be a passion for what the company is accomplishing, and along that journey, others will be inspired.

A few years ago, I read the book *Good to Great* by Jim Collins. I spent several sessions discussing the book with a group of entrepreneurs in a CEO forum that was established by the College of William & Mary. The book explores the difference between the characteristics of "good businesses" and those that were transformed from good to "great businesses." The book partially focuses on the leadership of the businesses and how the leadership shaped the transformation from good to great. "All the good-to-great companies had Level 5 leadership at the time of transition. Furthermore, the absence of Level 5 leadership showed up as a consistent pattern in the comparison companies." Collins states, "Level 5 leaders channel their ego needs away from themselves into the larger goal of building a great company. . . . It's not that Level 5 leaders have no ego or self-interest. Indeed, they are incredibly ambitions . . . but their ambition is first and foremost for the institution not themselves. . . . Level 5 leaders are a study in duality: modest and willful, humble and fearless."[32] Collins further describes the Level 5 Hierarchy as follows:

Level 5 Executive: Builds enduring greatness through a paradoxical blend of personal humility and professional will.
Level 4 Effective Leader: Catalyzes commitment to and vigorous pursuit of a clear and compelling vision, stimulating higher performance standards.
Level 3 Competent Manager: Organizes people and resources toward the effective and efficient pursuit of predetermined objectives.
Level 2 Contributing Team Member: Contributes individual capabilities to achievement of group objectives and works effectively with others in a group setting.

Level 1 Highly Capable Individual: Makes productive contributions through talent, knowledge, skills, and good work habits.

Collins states, "fully developed Level 5 leaders embody all five layers . . ."[33] I think what is most striking about the characteristics of a Level 5 leader is the humility that Collins speaks of. In this case, it is an important trait. Certainly, I would anticipate that the successful social entrepreneur would have a great deal of humility also.

Human resources are the most valuable asset to a business, and the "good to great" businesses seemed to realize and value that resource. However, I thought what was most fascinating was not just making sure that the right persons were on board; instead, it was making sure that the right persons were in the right positions to be the most effective. Trying to move forward "on the bus" with the wrong persons in the wrong seats can impact the bottom line.

Deepak Chopra, a spiritual leader, states in *The Soul of Leadership*, "A visionary leader won't be satisfied with building a team of competent, skilled people. Important as that surely is, it's even more vital to show the group—and the world at large—that your actions are authentic. Every time you stand up in a group, you affirm the truth voiced by Italo Magni, prize-winning public speaker: 'If you're talking with your head, you're going to speak to their heads. If you're talking with your heart, you're going to reach their hearts. If you talk with your life, you're going to reach their lives.' "[34]

Howard Schultz, CEO and chairman of Starbucks, said in an interview with Oprah Winfrey that he is driven by passion, that he is in business to exceed the expectation of the customer, and that it's not what you do, but why you do it. His focus on "Passion, Preparedness,

Leadership, and Compassion" has proven very effective. For example, his concern for his employees' well-being drove the decision to ensure they had good health insurance, even before the Affordable Care Act was enacted. Most businesses would have been more concerned about the bottom line. However, the well-being of the employees was important to him. Maybe his experience growing up as a kid in Brooklyn somehow impacted his decisions; nevertheless, his investment in the workforce has been a wise business strategy and part of the reason for the success of his company.

But you don't need to be a large business to make a difference. Most businesses in the United States are small businesses. According to the Small Business Administration, 99.7 percent of US employers are small entities. In 2011 there were 28.2 million small businesses. Since the latest recession, from mid-2009 to mid-2013, small firms accounted for 60 percent of the net new jobs.[35] But regardless of whether the business is large or small, each has the opportunity to contribute to society. The Bill and Melinda Gates Foundation is another great example of social entrepreneurship. The annual grant payments of the foundation in 2012 totaled $3.4 billion. The impact of the foundation over the years to develop solutions around the world for societies is insurmountable, ranging from the expansion of childhood immunizations, thus saving the lives of newborns, to increasing the income for small farmers in Africa, and making financial services available to the poor. Authors William D. Eggers and Paul Macmillan, in their book *The Solution Revolution*, calls this breed of leaders the "wavemakers": "For-profit, nonprofit, governmental organizations or individuals that revolutionize how the world approaches thorny social challenges. The wavemakers of the solution economy see old problems with new eyes. . . . Today private philanthropy to the developing world surpasses the monetary contributions of all governments combined."[36] The work of many of the leading companies today plays an important role in addressing the social issues around the world.

This topic may be reported annually in a company's Corporate Responsibility Report. For instance, Nike states, "Climate change is a critical issue . . . we seek to cut energy use and greenhouse gas (CO_2) emissions throughout our value chain, to reduce our climate impacts as well as energy-related costs. . . . We leverage the power of our employees, brands, consumers, and partners to support organizations and collaborations that create positive long-term changes that expand access to sport, empower adolescent girls in the developing world, and support the communities in which we live, work and play." In 2013, the company contributed $52.7 million in cash ($34.9) and ($17.8) product/in-kind.[37]

Other companies are equally committed to social responsibility. Coca-Cola, for instance, sees being recognized as a "responsible" company as part of its long-term business strategy: "What better way to be responsible than to recognize the issues that impact our society and develop solutions to address those issues to include: the workplace, environment, the community, and product responsibility. One key business strategy is to establish a sustainable water management model and . . . reduce the amount of water consumed per product in all operation fields."[38] Coke also reports the following to its stakeholders: "Water projects provide additional benefits, and initiatives for improving water access and sanitation alone have benefited 1.6 million people."[39]

Globally, social enterprises generated $2.1 trillion in revenue in 2012. In recent years, this number has grown by 15.1%

annually.[40] In 2013, more than 500 companies pledged over $2 billion in pro bono services. "A Billion + Change began in 2008, when more than 150 top corporate government and nonprofit leaders met at the White House for *The Summit on Corporate Volunteerism* to identify the benefits to companies of providing pro-bono and skills-based services." [41]

There is no shortage of the need for solutions to the growing demands in our country. For instance, the fastest-growing segment of our population is the segment of our population over 90 years old. Around the same time I started my first business, in 1994, my father was diagnosed with prostate cancer; a few years later he was diagnosed with lung cancer. Although I had been in the healthcare field all of my adult life, I felt completely inadequate to care for an aging parent. I wanted to make sure that he was getting the best care and to make sure my mom was supported as she would be involved, not just with his care but also with her own emotional strain. My experience came from my journey through that very difficult time. However, after my father passed in 2000, I realized that I would be confronted with the same situation as my mother aged, and I noted how ill-prepared we are as a nation to meet the needs of this growing elderly population. It was around that time that I was asked to join the Center for Excellence in Aging and Geriatric Health as a board member. The organization was founded as a research entity, created to improve the quality of life for the elderly. I thought of this as an excellent opportunity to offer my business experience, as well as insight from my own personal experience in caring for elderly parents. However, I could also learn from experts in the field of geriatric research and elderly health.

Many communities currently face, and will continue to face, growing demands for social services and programs to care for the elderly. This will continue to place a strain on local community resources and the traditional cost borne by, for example, Medicaid from nursing home placements. This trend is not likely to get any better as Americans are living longer. In the September 1998 issue of *American Journal of Public Health*, a study looked at the projection of future prevalence and incidents of Alzheimer's disease in the United States. Based on the results, the study reported these findings: "In 1997, the prevalence of Alzheimer's disease in the United States was 2.32 million with 68% being female. It was projected that the prevalence will nearly quadruple in the next 50 years by which time approximately 1 in 45 Americans will be afflicted with the disease. . . . The conclusion was that Alzheimer's disease will become an enormous public health problem, and interventions that could delay disease onset, even modestly, would have a major public health impact."[42]

Creative solutions to America's social issues will continue to be in high demand. Colleges and universities are taking note, such as Colorado State University's Global Social and Sustainable Enterprise MBA program, created to keep up with growing societal demands. Likewise, a national movement toward social entrepreneurship will also pick up speed, since there is an overwhelming need to address social problems–not just in the United States but throughout the world.

I met Dr. Clyde Oden Jr. in the 1990s. There are some people you never forget. Well, he was one of those persons. Often times our lives can be impacted by a single encounter.

Dr. Oden was a community leader, activist, CEO, physician, and minister with a MBA and other credentials. He was playing a significant role transforming the community of Watts in South Central Los Angeles in the 1990s. Long before the growing popularity of social entrepreneurship, he was using the model. He was president and CEO of Watts Health Systems, and I was a consultant to DHHS when we met in the 1990s as I visited the organization. The organization received funding to support healthcare initiatives in an underserved community. The area being served gained national attention in 1992 due to the Los Angeles riots. Many referred to the riots as the Rodney King Riots, where a series of civil disturbances and a string of arson crimes followed the acquittal of police officers on trial for brutality. (There was a videotaped police incident involving victim Rodney King.) From April 29 to May 4, National Guard soldiers patrolled Los Angeles. Over 50 deaths occurred and thousands were injured and arrested. The aftermath found a community in need of healing and transformation.

Although my visit occurred after the riots, I was struck by the connection this CEO had with the community. Plagued with poverty, unemployment, gang violence, and homelessness, this community benefitted from his model of "reach the people where they are," and this example really stuck with me. What I remember most are the lives in the community he seemed to have touched. As I talked to the community members–from former gang members and substance abusers to those who had been homeless–they wanted me to know he was their hero.

His organization had developed "wraparound services" to serve even the most basic needs of the individual. Someone who is homeless and hungry is not going to think much about healthcare. So the model was to feed them, clothe them, and find them shelter as their health issues were being treated. But it didn't stop there; it was about lifting up a people. They were taught entrepreneurial skills, like how to start businesses. Jazz festivals and community events were held to support local entrepreneurs. People came from across the country to the festivals and found beautiful artistic talents in the process. But wait, it didn't stop there either. There was a bank. An African-American-majority-owned bank was developed as part of this community redevelopment under the umbrella of the Watts Health Foundation. This was an effort to tap and support economic opportunities in South Central Los Angeles. Meeting this leader and having this experience many years ago was something I never forgot. It doesn't surprise me to know that he later moved on to pastor a church in the area with a large congregation. The ministries of the church have a common theme, similar to that of the foundation he led: transformation, empowerment, and the common good.

CHAPTER 6

It's *All* about the Relationship

Be humble and gentle. Be patient with each other, making allowance for each other's faults because of your love. Try always to be led along together by the Holy Spirit and so be at peace with one another. We are all parts of one body, we have the same Spirit, and we have all been called to the same glorious future. For us there is only one Lord, one faith, one baptism, and we all have the same God and Father who is over us all and in us all, and living through every part of us.

—Ephesians 4:2-7

Regardless of our profession or social circles, the relationships we develop will be invaluable. Without establishing relationships, there can be no common good. If business owners do not establish and maintain relationships with customers through excellent customer service, this will definitely impact their bottom line. If relationships are not established with employees, this will impact employee satisfaction and can ultimately impact the bottom line. If pastors and church leaders do not establish relationships with church congregants, they may see membership decline. Sometimes we devalue another in our life only to realize later that his presence had a particular purpose—one we were not able to recognize at the time. Each person who comes into our lives is there to teach us something. Many are surprised by that. But because we do not know the path of our unique journeys, that individual could very well be the person who one day saves your life. Even the most stormy relationships or encounters have a purpose.

In relationships, we learn not just about others but also about ourselves. Others bring out the best in us—or the worst. Either way, they can bring out the raw emotions that we sometimes hold inside. These experiences are part of the journey to create awareness, and they provide opportunities for learning. Others cannot bring out what is not already inside of us. When someone says, "Oh, that person just makes me so angry; they bring out the worst in me, and I say things that I shouldn't say," then the good news might be that you are in touch with your emotions—sometimes even suppressed emotions buried deep in the subconscious. What are the triggers or the things that make us "crazy" and why? So is it the other person, or is it the unresolved feelings within us, such as prejudices or hurt from painful past experiences? Maybe that person who just made you crazy actually helped you learn something about yourself. On the contrary, many people come into our lives and are like "rays of sunshine," creating feelings of peacefulness and calm.

Much of the stress in our life is self-induced. A simple example that I learned was about "control." When we try to control the behavior of others or situations in our life, it becomes very frustrating when we cannot get our way. We feel like we are losing control or losing something, and that frustration escalates into feelings of lack and, ultimately, anger or depression. Whenever this happens, we must take a step back and ask ourselves this question: What is the worst thing that could happen? It really puts things in perspective. This makes us appreciate even the small things.

If we learned to appreciate and respect the beauty of the diversity in our country, life would be much less stressful. Just like the success of a marriage means working at the relationship, the same is true for the leaders of our country. Representatives and senators must establish relationships and get to know the constituents that they represent. The gridlock in Washington is because we have lost interest in the common good of the people. The common good of the American people has been turned into a political football game, with getting re-elected as the goal line.

Pastor Joel Osteen states in *Your Best Life Now*, "God is not going to change anyone you are dealing with until he first changes you. But if you'll quit complaining about everybody around you and, instead, start taking a good look inside and working with God to change you, God will change those other people. Examine your own heart and see if there are attitudes and motives that you need to change." [43] Nothing could describe this better than the transformation that occurs with a butterfly. There is a natural process that occurs, and isn't it amazing that the caterpillar at each stage of its transformation knows how to prepare? He is not learning this from a textbook, but he is just "allowing" his transformation to happen naturally. As a caterpillar, he eats the leaves and grows bigger. He then starts to shed the skin and eventually stops eating as he prepares to hang upside down from a leaf or branch. The caterpillar spins and forms a cocoon to protect himself, starting the journey of transformation inside the cocoon, literally transforming his body. When ready, he emerges as a beautiful and radiant butterfly. The irony is that he was always a butterfly, but the transformation is what allows others to see what was there all along. Everything that happened to the caterpillar was "preprogramed" by the Creator. The only thing the insect did was to embrace the process.

There are tools we can use to work on ourselves and aid our transformation. For instance, emotional intelligence is one tool. Emotional intelligence means asking ourselves questions as we assess our emotions and the emotions of others with whom we are interacting. It means assessing how we feel and how they feel. Emotional intelligence is often used in business and social circles to guide decisions. This opens the door to creating an emotional connection. Emotional intelligence is helpful in building lasting relationships. It moves us away from the quest for dictatorship and from feelings of anger because someone does not agree with our point of view. Instead, emotional intelligence helps us to understand others' views, behaviors, and actions.

We cannot talk about emotional intelligence without talking about spiritual intelligence. According to Stephen Covey, "Spiritual intelligence is the central and most fundamental of all the intelligences, because it becomes the source of guidance for the others." [44] We have to ask ourselves these questions: How do we inspire others when we are not inspired? How do we motivate others toward a positive change when we do not feel motivated?

The people we attract into our life are more like us than we may be willing to admit. It is possible that our words may not be a reflection of who we are or how we feel. We are speaking words from our conscious thoughts; however, there are subconscious thoughts that we may not even realize are there. Even our subconscious thoughts and feelings can impact our lives and those of others around us. If we do not have positive relationships in our life, we must first ask ourselves, "Why am I attracting the people that I am attracting? What is it about me that draws people in my life that are not good for me?"

If the wrong types of people seem to show up in your life, then you must simply ask yourself what kind of "energy" you are projecting– even unknowingly. I had a friend in college who, in later years, had a devastating experience. She was happily engaged to be married to the man of her dreams. He was a religious leader, and she had met him through one of her childhood friends who attended his church. It was love at first sight. During that time, she had suffered losses in her life, including the loss of her mother and an aunt, both of whom she had helped to care for. Somehow with this new relationship, she felt that things were looking up in her life. I mean, who wouldn't feel that? She attended his church services. They grew closer, and she trusted him. She was generous, so when he told her his dream of starting a ministry, she did not think twice about helping him. She invested time and eventually money. When she called and told me she was engaged, I was happy for her. She asked me to be in the wedding, and I was honored.

Then the unthinkable happened. It was one week before the wedding. I will never forget that three a.m. phone call; she was crying hysterically. I asked her, "What has you so upset?" There I was on the phone with this strong, independent woman who could barely get out the words, "He called it off! He called off the wedding." The phone went silent; then there was a gasp for air. "Oh, my God, what happened?" I managed to say. I mean, was this merely a case of wedding jitters? Perhaps no one will ever know the real reason. He was gone, but how could she not have seen this coming? Years of private investigators and money spent turned up nothing. Please do not get this wrong. There is no excuse for his behavior; however, does our spirit not speak to us about relationships or sometimes tell us things we are not willing or wanting to hear? One might conclude that even our emotional state can affect our emotional intelligence and what we are able to perceive about others.

Dr. Wayne W. Dyer says, "Trust in your own greatness. You are not this body you occupy, which is temporary and on its way back to the nowhere from which it came. You are pure greatness . . . precisely the very same greatness that creates all of life. Keep this thought uppermost in your mind, and you'll attract to yourself these same powers of creation: The right people will appear. The exact events that you desire will transpire. The financing will show up. That's because greatness attracts more of its own self to itself, just as thoughts of inadequacy act upon a belief that ensures that deficiency will become a reality."[45]

Whether it's personal or business, relationships are important. I started this book by stating that we attract who we are, but when there is a hole in your heart created by loss or other life experiences, it is much easier to attract the wrong people in your life. But it is in those darkest times in our life that true friendships are the most important. Find someone you know you can trust, and seek professional help if necessary. No one should have to go it alone.

However, with all that being said, the experiences we encounter are part of our life's journey. Good or bad, people who come into our lives are there to teach us something about ourselves. Know that, even as we grow spiritually, we may simply outgrow some friendships and gain new friendships, since most of the time the people around us are a reflection of who we are. Therefore, as you change, the people closest to you will also change. They are our mirrors.

Attract the right relationships by first seeking inner peace through prayer, meditation, and quiet time. Forgive yourself for past mistakes, and heal the wounds of the past. Sometimes it's a traumatic childhood, sometimes an abusive relationship; the universe around you is responding to your state of mind, and if there is a void, it's important not just to fill the void with busyness, but to deal with the underlying feelings.

A meaningful purpose is the aspiration of every living soul. But we must first understand "who" we are to understand "why" we are here. Having this inner peace and "knowing" on the inside will shape what happens to us on the outside. We do not have to be defined by what is happening around us, but instead, we should feel a sense of calm, an anchoring inside ourselves–even in the storms. When we are aligned with the Creator of all things, that knowing seems to come easier.

When I was a freshman in college, I took an anthropology course in summer school. I really liked the professor. He made what I thought might be a very boring topic very exciting. He was young, energetic, and so enthusiastic about the subject. When I returned to school in the fall semester, I returned to the news that this anthropology professor had drowned over the summer. I was devastated. Evidently, he went to the beach and was out swimming when he got caught up in a rip current. Even the most conditioned swimmers can hardly sustain a fight against a rip current. Conventional wisdom is to allow the current to take you out and away from the shore, and when you no longer feel the pull of the water, then swim back to shore. When I thought about the strength and the pull of these rip currents, it was a reminder of what the storms in our life feel like. Perhaps even the same wisdom would apply. Instead of fighting against the storm, just anchor down, and ride it out. It will pass.

Your heavenly Father already knows all your needs and he will give you all you need from day to day if you live for him and make the Kingdom of God your primary concern.
—Matthew 6:32-33

If we are not able to build relationships for the common good, then it has to be because we are living within our egos, and we must understand that our ego is not who we are. It is not our true self, which is created by the Creator and is far more powerful than the ego. Humility has power.

We should live our lives, not pursuing what's in it for us, but asking how we can be of service to others. If we are one in God, the Divine, then we should be about service. We should have reverence for every human being, and we should expect the same respect from others. When we start expecting people to treat us indifferently, then they will; but even if they treat us unkindly, we must remember it is not about us. What is most helpful when it comes to getting to know others is something very simple. My experiences have led me to believe that there are two dominate feelings: love and fear. When we look at each of these emotions, we can see that many other feelings originate from either fear or love. Once I understood this, it changed the way I looked at and reacted to the actions of others. I believe that we either operate out of love or out of fear, and many of the emotions we encounter every day come from one of those two places.

With fear:	hatred, anger, anxiety, irritation, loneliness, mean-spiritedness, bitterness
With love:	joy, compassion, enjoyment, pleasure, kindness, empathy

Bitterness, anger, and anxiety are all emotions that stem from underlying fear. Fear sometimes stands in the way of creating meaningful relationships. Fear comes from separation from the "Source," and we might sense a lack of grounding or assurance. Remember the drop of water that will dry up once separated from its source, the ocean? The same is true for humans. Decisions we make may keep us on the same course or move us in a different direction. It's not only important to make a decision, but also to understand why you are making a particular decision. Faith has to be greater than the fear. Consider the biblical story of Peter observing Jesus walking on water:

> *Immediately Jesus made the disciples get into the boat and go on ahead of him to the other side, while he dismissed the crowd. After he had dismissed them, he went up on a mountainside by himself to pray. Later that night, he was there alone, and the*

boat was already a considerable distance from land, buffeted by the waves because the wind was against it. Shortly before dawn Jesus went out to them, walking on the lake. When the disciples saw him walking on the lake, they were terrified. "It's a ghost," they said, and cried out in fear. But Jesus immediately said to them: "Take courage! It is I. Don't be afraid." "Lord, if it's you," Peter replied, "tell me to come to you on the water." "Come," he said. Then Peter got down out of the boat, walked on the water and came toward Jesus. But when he saw the wind, he was afraid and, beginning to sink, cried out, "Lord, save me!" Immediately Jesus reached out his hand and caught him. "You of little faith," he said, "why did you doubt?"
        —Matthew 14:22-31

Peter and those on the boat are afraid at first, but once Peter hears the voice of Jesus, he takes a leap of faith and steps off the boat, and he begins to walk on water. However, the fear returns when he starts looking around at the wind and the waves. He then cries out for Jesus to save him, and he is saved. It is really faith that keeps us "walking on the water," even when the wind and the waves are pounding around us.

When I see people who are mean-spirited and angry, to me that screams **FEAR**. So instead of reacting to their anger, ask yourself instead: What are they afraid of? What are the experiences of their journey that have made them fearful? What's behind the anger? When we are not feeling well and go to the doctor, we go because of the symptoms we are having; however, the doctor seeks to find the underlying condition, based on the symptoms that have manifested. I bet if you got to know that person with so much hatred, you would learn that fear was the underlying condition behind the hate.

On the other hand, it does not take much to feel the love of the person who shows compassion and kindness. Love breeds happiness and joy. We are all connected to the same Source, so we already have a connection with one another. Therefore, we can feel the energy of people around us. When we are operating from a state of love, there is a true sense of power since love is more powerful than fear. We can start to change the atmosphere around us, including the people around us. Remember, God is love, and "perfect love casts out all fear." (1 John 4:18) Even science is proving this to be true, as studies show more illnesses associated with fear and anger, and greater health benefits associated with love and spiritual connection.

Scientifically, the energy field associated with light moves much faster than that of darkness, which is a slower-moving energy field. We remember that principle from science class. But imagine a pole lying on the ground, with fear on one end and love on the other. Imagine the end of the pole with fear also shows darkness, and as you move along the pole toward the opposite end, where love is present, you begin to move toward the light. So the more we move toward love, the brighter our light shines; likewise, the further we move from the light into darkness, the more we become engulfed with fear. The Source is our light, and a separation from the Source will lead to a life dominated by fear. Our journey here on this earth is to find how to move out of darkness into the light of love. It is not unnatural to feel fear; fear can sometimes be a motivator to understand what is going on underneath—in other words, our true feelings. It is a trigger to help understand what is underneath the fear. Embrace the fear. Understand it, and move through it. The fear and absence of love in the world creates havoc for the entire world. Remember what Paul writes to Timothy: "For God hath not given us the spirit of fear; but of power, and of love, and of a sound mind." (2 Tim. 1:7)

Suppose someone is saying all of the right things, even sometimes speaking very positively, but hiding how he is really feeling. You instinctively feel something different. The Holy Spirit allows us to feel that difference. When we are connected to the Spirit, we have a gift we can tap into called a "discerning spirit." A discerning spirit helps us to know whether something is of God. An awareness starts to develop, and we start to see things with new eyes. We can even change the atmosphere around us by projecting love and compassion.

I have decided to stick with love. Hate is too great a burden to bear.

—Dr. Martin Luther King Jr.

If you walk into the office in the morning at work and a coworker walks past you, snaps at you rudely, and continues to walk by, you can go from a state of happiness to anger at an amazing speed. However, know that it is your **choice** to rush to anger. That person's bad attitude is not about you. Our choices can have a ripple effect, so make the right choice. The choice that you make will not only affect you, but all those around you.

Jesus described the relationship his disciples are to have with the world. They are to be the "salt of the earth" (Matthew 5:13 KJV), keeping the world from spoiling or being tasteless; they are to be the "light of the world" (Matthew 5:14), providing light for the pathway of men who would otherwise stumble along in darkness. He said to "love your enemies, bless them that curse you, and do good to them that hate you, and pray for them which despitefully use you and persecute you" (Matthew 5:44 KJV). This is the "Kingdom" culture, and it embraces others.

Jesus said, "Thou shalt love the Lord your God with all your heart and with all your soul and with all your mind. This is the first and great commandment. And the second is like unto it: Thou shalt love your neighbor as thyself. On these two commandments hang all the law and the prophets."
—Matthew 22:37-40 KJV

I once met a woman from a large metropolitan area, a retired executive from IBM. She started a technology company after retirement. When we say that each of us has a purpose, well this woman's story definitely speaks to her purpose. Armed with a passion for helping women, she invested in transitional housing for homeless women and children. Many times she found herself out on the street in the bitter cold, rounding up women who were sleeping on the street with their children. She would take them first to the hospital, and later to the transitional housing that she owned to get them cleaned up. She never told many people what she was doing. Most thought, as I did, that she was just someone who had retired from corporate America and had started a new business. People knew her by day, but few knew her purpose and how she spent her nights on the street. However, her passion and compassion for helping women, specifically the homeless, moved her into action.

Real change happens when "believers" are moving in their faith. If we want change, we have to create it. Change might start small for some; it might be serving those in our households or helping our neighbors. Or, service might happen in the communities in which we live. We might get more involved in the political process to stand up for what is best for the country. These are just a few ways every human being can create a personal agenda called the "common good."

Several years ago, I was a founding member of a grassroots organization called ALLTOGETHER. The organization was founded locally after the Rodney King verdict in Los Angeles, when racial tensions were escalating across the country. Since then, we have seen the same tensions in Ferguson, Missouri, with the shooting of a black, unarmed 18-year old teenager by a white police officer, and in Baltimore when a young black man died while in the custody of the police. ALLTOGETHER was and is designed to foster cultural awareness and harmony, as well as provide a forum for the community to communicate across racial lines. The hope is to foster unity, inclusiveness, and equal opportunity, thereby improving the quality of life for all citizens in the community.

ALLTOGETHER was truly my first experience with such an initiative. We began with community forums to highlight or create an awareness of the disparities in the community along racial and socioeconomic lines in the areas of education, housing, economics, and healthcare. We even held a religious forum where religious leaders from across the community participated. Someone made the point that the most segregated time in our nation and community is eleven a.m. on Sunday morning (referring to church worship services). Our intent was to look at disparities in the community, supported by data, and to engage the community in these discussions.

We had to start by creating an awareness. How can we solve problems if we are not willing to have an open dialogue? Study circles were facilitated to discuss candidly our attitudes and personal feelings about race and racism. The small study groups were diverse across racial and socioeconomics lines. Race was discussed openly, including our own personal experiences growing up and what we were taught about race. Lasting relationships were formed and bridges were built that were instrumental in developing a platform for the common good in the community. Until we are willing to have hard discussions, it will be difficult to build the bridges that are needed to unite our country.

A nation cannot allow income disparity or injustice to hamper its growth and potential. There has to be national, state, and local leadership with "heart." Deepak Chopra states in *The Soul of Leadership*, "Leading from the soul means taking responsibility for more than the group's needs. It means having concern for everyone's personal growth. This responsibility begins with your own evolution." Chopra also says that "in eight areas of your life you have the power to be guided by your soul: thoughts, emotions, perception, personal relationships, social roles, environment, speech, and the body. In all these areas, your behavior affects the people you lead. If you evolve, so will they."[46]

Intention could be described as having a strong will or purpose in life. When speaking of intention, Dr. Wayne Dyer writes in *The Power of Intention*, "Over the past quarter of a century, however, I've felt a shift in my thinking from a purely psychological or personal growth emphasis, toward a spiritual orientation where healing, creating miracles, manifesting, and making a connection to divine intelligence are genuine possibilities."[47]

God, or the Source, is omnipresent, everywhere. This means he is not a God of some, but of all. He is not separate from us.

Growing up, I remember God was often described as if he sat somewhere watching you, waiting for you to make mistakes so that he could punish you. But the journey is about learning, and now my thoughts have changed over the years. I feel that the Spirit, or the Source, connects us one to another. The only thing that gets in the way sometimes is our egos. When we are controlled by ego, it is difficult, if not impossible, to feel a true connection with others. The more we are able to open our minds and our hearts, the more we are able to connect with the Spirit and with each other. It is really about loving others and knowing that peace cannot be realized if we feel separate from one another.

Some might say, "I can live without him or her," or maybe, "I don't need anyone." Then I would say that you will live and die a very lonely life. We were not created to be alone or excluded from the rest of society. Statistically, it has even been found that couples in loving relationships or individuals who are socially active tend to have a longer life expectancy than those who live alone or tend to exclude themselves from society.

It is not nonviolence if we merely love those that love us. It is nonviolence only when we love those that hate us. I know how difficult it is to follow this grand law of love. But are not all great and good things difficult to do? Love of the hater is the most difficult of all. But by the grace of God even this most difficult thing becomes easy to accomplish if we want to do it.

—Gandhi

Listen to Your Heart: The Ukrainian Experience

When asked to go to Ukraine, I had mixed feelings. Ukraine had partnered with the US Centers for Disease Control and a major American university and was planning to launch a monitoring and evaluation process of their healthcare centers Ukraine wanted to learn more about the monitoring and evaluation process that had been developed by the US government to evaluate many of the federally funded programs in the United States. I have always believed that when we are able to exchange ideas with other countries, it is, undoubtedly, a learning experience for all parties.

Normally, being the only African American on a team would not have mattered to me; however, this was not just any place. This was Ukraine. "Following the collapse of czarist Russia in 1917, Ukraine was able to achieve a short-lived period of independence (1917-1920), but was reconquered and forced to endure a brutal Soviet rule that engineered two forced famines (1921-1922 and 1932-1933) in which over 8 million died. In World War II, German and Soviet armies were responsible for some 7 to 8 million more deaths." Final independence was achieved in 1991 with the dissolution of the Union of Soviet Socialist Republics (USSR) ...The country is slightly smaller than Texas, but with a population estimate at 44,573,205, according to The World Factbook.... While very rich in natural resources, nearly 24 percent of the country is below the federal poverty line ...The religion is overwhelmingly Christian, and up to two-thirds of the people identify themselves as Orthodox.".[48] The percentage of blacks is said to be less than 1 percent. That must be the case, as I saw very few blacks, maybe six total, during my three weeks of traveling the country. Nevertheless, I was very intrigued with the idea of learning a new culture and getting to know the people.

I was not quite sure what to expect, although I did plenty of research and even learned a bit of Russian before traveling, not wanting to rely totally on translators. (In the areas I traveled, both Russian and Ukrainian were spoken.) I decided to go to the "blogosphere" to see what travelers to the region were saying about the culture—especially about blacks visiting the country. According to an article in the *Kyiv Post*, "As for racial attacks in mostly white Ukraine, the numbers are hopeful: From 2006-2008, 184 attacks and 12 racially-motivated murders took place. In 2009, no racial murders were recorded and only 40 such incidents of violence were reported ... foreign students of African or Asian origin are the most common targets of xenophobic attacks and abuse in Ukraine."[49] This was not exactly what I wanted to hear. But I also remembered reading one comment in a blog from someone in the country who said this: "The real problem is that we have never had an opportunity to get to know blacks, and there is always fear associated with what you do not know." That struck a note with me. In some strange way, that comment made sense to me. We cannot change people's perceptions by buying into the stereotype. It did not mean that I did not have concerns; however, I chose to believe, instead, that, in general, people respond to fear with fear and people respond to love and kindness with love and kindness.

When we arrived in Ukraine, we were picked up at the airport. While there might have been stares, I did not particularly notice that the stares were just at me, but my colleagues as well. The three weeks seemed to breeze by, and travel throughout the country was beyond belief: by car, bus, and the overnight train. The countryside, with fields of plush green and crops as far as you could see, was breathtaking. From the capital of Kiev to the city of Odessa on the shores of the Black Sea, and Dnipropetrovsk, our travel was escorted by the Ukrainian team members, including some from the Ukrainian government. The three wonderful translators who traveled with us were always on their game. Sometimes we would find ourselves so caught up in the moment that I or a Ukrainian member would be speaking in our native language, totally forgetting that we needed a translator. We would smile and then turn around to find one of the translators to help us out. We bonded.

They wanted the best for their country and wanted to make sure they had good systems in place to evaluate their HIV/AIDS health programs. They knew that we (United States) had established evaluation practices for health programs that they could learn from, and possibly adopt, to increase capacity and efficiency in the regional health centers.

I could not help but think how far things had come between the two countries in terms of their relationship. But what was it like during the Cold War, when Ukraine was part of the former Soviet Union? How had they perceived the United States? I was curious, but dared not ask. My answer came anyway. One of the most interesting stories is from a conversation I had with one of the translators. As we walked out of the restaurant, heading back to one of the medical clinics, he pointed to a shelter on the side of the street that looked like an underground bunker. He said, "The children were taught how to protect themselves; they had drills in school to prepare in the event that the US dropped a bomb. We knew exactly what to do." To me, it was confirmation of how far we had come, but also a reminder of the effects of war and how it changes the lives of so many. He then asked me, "What did you do in the US? Did you practice drills in school to prepare for a possible attack by the Soviets?" Trying not to be a smart aleck, but wanting not to revisit the Cold War, I said, "If we did, I must have missed those classes." He just looked at me and started to laugh.

Once I was back in the United States, I remember having a conversation about my experiences in Ukraine and whether I experienced any discrimination or animosity while in the country. Well, I think the last meeting and my debriefing spoke volumes about the success of my experience. We met with other key Ukrainian stakeholders on the last day of the visit to present the results of our findings and our recommendations. As I spoke, the translation was simultaneous, so I did not have to wait for my words to be translated. For me, this moment really summed up the experience. I got two thumbs-up, indicating agreement, from the Ukrainian travel team after my final presentation to the group. The success of the visit was due to the hard work of the Ukrainian team to make sure that our stay was comfortable and safe. The raw emotions of the goodbyes were so heartfelt; an emotional connection had developed at some level. Even with reservations, I felt that it was a journey I was meant to take; but I could not make it about me. I needed to go with my authentic self—not as an African American or with ego or judgment or condemnation or fear. I had to go knowing that we were all created in the image of God.

Dr. Wayne Dyer states in *Change Your Thoughts–Change Your Life,* "Make compassion the essential foundation of your personal philosophy. Feeling guilty about what you've amassed or wallowing in sadness over the plight of the striving won't change things, but making compassion the essential foundation of your philosophy will. This is one of the most significant ways of initiating the growth of a critical mass. As that mass grows, kind hearts and actions will realign our planet: Likeminded leaders will emerge, and gross inconsistencies will be reduced and eventually eliminated. Mother Teresa was an outstanding example of how one person's way of seeing the world can change the world itself: 'In each person,' she said, 'I see the face of Christ in one of his more distressing disguises.' " [50]

It serves us well to put loving thoughts in our minds about the people in our life. Remember: The more you change the way you look at things, the more the things you look at will change. Handle situations without judgment. This reminds me of a young lady that I met about a year ago. However, before I met her, her reputation had preceded her. I was told that she was very difficult to get along with and had a condescending attitude. Of course, I had never met her, but when you have several persons who are saying the same thing, it does get your attention. However, despite being told all of those things, I wanted to keep an open mind. We decided to meet in the hotel for dinner the evening of our arrival in the city to prepare for a program assessment the following day.

At dinner, often if I asked a question, she would come back with an answer that was more of a lecture than a simple answer to the question. If I offered a suggestion, there would always be an alternative that, of course, she felt was a better option. I paid close attention and decided that there was either something making her feel threatened, or she was just having a bad day. I wondered, *What is really underneath the sarcasm and the snarled remarks?*

At the hotel that evening as we retired to our rooms, I asked her if she would join me for breakfast the next morning. It would be the first time that she and I would be alone. At breakfast, I asked her to tell me something about herself, and she did. People generally like talking about themselves. I started talking about my mom, as

I often do, saying that caring for an aging parent is rewarding and challenging at the same time. Well, somehow that struck a nerve, and she began sharing some of her story. She had family members who had suffered with Alzheimer's. She was certain that one day she would end up with Alzheimer's too; in fact, she had already starting preparing for that day. She made scrapbooks with pictures, so that in later years it would jog her memory about some of the good times. I could hardly believe what I was hearing. As I said before, all of your actions in life are either coming from a place of fear or a place of love. Certainly, her actions and attitudes were coming from a place of fear. I felt that a window just opened in our very new relationship, and before the end of the week, a door had opened.

I understood—it was never about me. Many times, we want to give ourselves far too much credit, making other people's moods all about us. I just know that I left that week feeling really happy that I did not get caught up in the spiderweb of gossip, but instead was able to stay grounded in what my spirit was telling me about the person. Relationships are priceless, but the message from the poem "ANYWAY" is the best way to deal with the difficult ones. A version of this was said to be on Mother Teresa's wall. According to Lucinda Vardey, in *Mother Teresa: A Simple Path* (New York: Ballantine Books, 1995), page 185, there was "a sign on the wall of Shishu Bhavan, the children's home in Calcutta."

ANYWAY

People are unreasonable, illogical, and self-centered,

Love them anyway.

If you do good, people will accuse you of selfish ulterior motives.
Do good anyway.

If you are successful, you will win false friends and true enemies.
Succeed anyway.

The good you do will be forgotten tomorrow.
Do good anyway.

Honesty and frankness make you vulnerable.
Be honest and frank anyway.

What you spend years building may be destroyed overnight.
Build anyway.

People really need help but may attack you if you do help them.
Help people anyway.

Give the world the best you have and you'll get kicked in the teeth.
Give the world the best you've got anyway. [51]

Epilogue

We are our brother's keeper, and we do have a responsibility to advocate for the common good. This is not difficult to believe if we understand how we are all connected. Understanding the connection of spiritual energy that exists in each of us is a start. The passion inside of you is really God's way of speaking to you and validating your purpose. Sometimes all you have to do is show up for the class. The manifestation of whatever you are looking for will show up; it's all in your mind, literally. Just believe it to receive it. We have to be the change we want to see in others.

Your stories and your experiences are all part of your journey. I would encourage everyone to write about the people you've met along the way who have made a difference in your life and/or are making a difference in their communities. There are many, and their work will not be in vain. If the American people and our Congress should take anything away from this text, it is that the common good never was and should never be political. The common good should be not *whether* but *how* we support a movement and inspire others to get involved. It is a message for politicians, entrepreneurs, businessmen, religious leaders, community leaders, youth, and families. We can all make a difference: one heart, one mind, one thought at a time. It's a new dawn. The time is now.

Bibliography

2001 Census and The World Factbook, CIA, https://www.cia.gov/
library/publications/the-world-factbook/geos/print/country/
countrypdf up.pdf.

Bishaw, Alemayehu and Kayla Fontenot. "Poverty: 2012 and
2013, American Community Survey Briefs." September
2014, http://www.census.gov/content/dam/Census/library/
publications/2014/acs/acsbr13   -01.pdf).

Brookmeyer, Ron, Sarah Gray, and Claudia Kawas. "Projections of
Alzheimer's Disease in the United States and the Public Health
Impact of Delaying Disease Onset." *American Journal Public
Health*, (September, 1998), http://www.ncbi.nlm.nih.gov/pmc/
articles/instance/1509089/.

Burstein, David D. *Fast Future: How the Millennial Generation Is
Shaping Our World*. Boston: Beacon Press, 2013.

Cecere, David, Cambridge Health Alliance, *Harvard Gazette*,
September 17, 2009, http://news.harvard.edu/gazette/

story/2009/09/new-study-finds-45000-deaths-annually-linked-to-lack-of-health-coverage/.

Census Data 2012.

Cetron, Marvin J. and Owen Davies. "52 Trends Shaping Tomorrow's World: Economic and Social Trends and Their Impacts." *The Futurist* (May/June 2010).

Chopra, Deepak. *The Soul of Leadership.* New York: Harmony Books, 2010.

Coca-Cola Corporate Social Responsibility Report, 2011.

Coca-Cola Corporate Sustainability Report/Water Stewardship, 2011/2012.

Coleman-Jensen, Alisha and Mark Nord. "Household Food Security in the United States in 2010." United States Department of Agriculture Economic Research Service, September 2011, http://www.ers.usda.gov/publications/err-economic-research-report/err125.aspx.

Coleman-Jensen, Alisha. "Household Food Security." USDA Economic Research Report Number 173, September 2014, www.ers.usda.gov (www.ers.usda.gov/publications/err-economic-research-report/err173.aspx).

Collins, Jim. *Good To Great, Why Some Companies Make the Leap . . . and Others Don't.* New York: HarperCollins 2001.

Covey, Stephen. *The 8th Habit: From Effectiveness to Greatness.* New York: Simon & Schuster, 2004.

Department of Health and Human Services (DHHS), Healthy People 2020.

Desilver, Drew. "Who's poor in America? 50 years into the 'War on Poverty,' a data portrait." Pew Research Center, January 13, 2014 (http://pewrsr.ch/1cWtBk1).

Kristof, Nicholas. "An Idiot's Guide to Inequality." *New York Times* (July 24, 2014).

Macartney, Suzanne. "Poverty Rates for Selected Detailed Race and Hispanic Groups by State and Place: 2007-2011." *American Community Survey Briefs*, November 2011, www.census.gov/ prod/acbr11-17.pdf.

Mather, Mark. "U.S. Children in Single-Mother Families." *Population Reference Bureau*, May 2010, www.prb.org/ Publications/Policy Briefs/singlemotherfamilies.aspx."Medical Expenditure Panel Survey," *Agency for Healthcare Research and Quality*, www.meps.ahrq.gov/mepsweb/.

Macartney, Suzanne. "Child Poverty in the United States 2009 and 2010: Selected Race Groups and Hispanic Origin." *American Community Survey Briefs*, November 2011, www.census.gov/ prod/2013/pubs/acsbr11-17.pdf.

"Millennials: A Portrait of Generation Next." *Pew Research Center*, Feb. 24, 2010. www.pewresearch.org/millenials. http://www. pewsocialtrends.org/files/2010/10/millennials-confident-connected-open-to-change.pdf.

Munroe, Myles. *A Kingdom Book: God's Big Idea*. Shippensburg, PA: Destiny Image Publishers, 2008.

National Coalition for the Homeless. "Homeless Youth." June 2008.

NikeInc. FY12/13 Sustainable Business Performance Summary. http://www.nikeresponsibility.com/report/uploads/files/FY12-13_NIKE_Inc_CR_Report.pdf

Nixon, Ron. "Farm Bill Compromise Will Change Programs and Reduce Spending," New York Times (January 27, 2014),

Devas-Walt, Carmen. "Income and Health Insurance Coverage in the United States: 2012"; Current Population Reports, US Department of Commerce, Economics and Statistics Administration, US Census Bureau, September 2013.

Dyer, Wayne W. *Change Your Thoughts—Change Your Life: Living the Wisdom of the Tao.* New York: Hay House, 2007.

Dyer, Wayne W. *The Power of Intention.* New York, Hay House, 2008.

Dyer, Wayne W., *The Shift*, directed by Michael Goorjian, executive producer Reid Tracy. Hay House DVD.

Eggers, William, and Paul Macmillan. *The Solution Revolution: How Business, Government, and Social Enterprises are Teaming up to Solve Society's Toughest Problems.* Boston: *Harvard Business Review Press*, 2013.

Friedman, Howard "America's Poverty-Education Link." *The Huffington Post*, October 29, 2012, www.huffingtonpost.com.

Gordon, David, Dr., University of Bristol, "Indicators of Poverty & Hunger," December 12-14, 2005. http://www.un.org/esa/socdev/unyin/documents/ydiDavidGordon_poverty.pdf.

Gunders, Dana. "Your Scraps Add Up: Reducing food waste can save money and resources." Natural Resources Defense Council, March 2013.

"HIV in the United States: At a Glance." Centers for Disease Control and Prevention. November 2014, http://www.cdc.gov/hiv/pdf/statistics_basics_ataglance_factsheet.pdf.

"Homeless Youth," National Coalition for the Homeless, factsheet published June 2008. http://nationalhomeless.org/factsheets/youth.html.

http://www.nytimes.com/2014/01/28/us/politics/farm-bill-compromise-will-reduce-spending-and-change-programs.html.

Osteen, Joel. *Your Best Life Now.* New York: Warner Faith, 2004.

Peters, Gerhard, and John T. Woolley. "Special Message to the Congress Proposing a Nationwide War on the Sources of Poverty." *The American Presidency Project*, March 16, 1964, www.presidency.ucsb.ed/ws/?pid=26109.

"Poverty and Its Measurement: The Presentation of a Range of Methods to Obtain Measures of Poverty," *Instituto Nacional de Estadistica*, 2009, www.ine.es/en/daco/daco42/sociales/pobreza_en.pdf.

Prymachyk, Iryna. "Reports of racist attacks down, but problem persists." *Kyiv Post* (April 21, 2010).

Small Business Administration SBA, Office of Advocacy, March 2014.

"The State of the World's Children," *UNICEF*, 2010, www.unicef.org/sowc/.

USDA statistics, 2012.http://ers.usda.gov/data-products/county-level-data-sets/poverty.aspx.

Vardey, Lucinda. *Mother Teresa, A Simple Path,* (New York: Ballantine Books, 1995).

Woolf , Steven H., and Laudan Aron, Editors. "U.S. Health in International Perspective Shorter Lives, Poorer Health." National Research Council and Institute of Medicine, The National Academies Press. Copyright 2013. http://obssr.od.nih.gov/pdf/IOM%20Report.pdf.

World Health Organization "Child marriages: 39,000 every day," March 7, 2013, http://www.who.int/mediacentre/news/releases/2013/child_marriage_20130307/en/.

http://mlk-kpp01.stanford.edu/kingweb/additional_resources
/articles/gospel.
http://siteresources.worldbank.org/INTPOVERTY/
Resources/335642-1124115102975/1555199-
1124115187705/ch2.pdf.
http://www.abillionpluschange.org.

Endnotes

1   http://mlk-kpp01.stanford.edu/kingweb/additional_resources/
    articles/gospel.

2   Carmen DeNavas-Walt, "Income and Health Insurance
    Coverage in the United States: 2012; Current Population
    Reports," US Department of Commerce, Economics and
    Statistics Administration, US Census Bureau, September 2013,
    23.

3   Dana Gunders, "Your Scraps Add Up: Reducing food waste can
    save money and resources" Natural Resources Defense Council,
    March 2013, 1.

4   Alisha Coleman-Jensen, "Household Food Security," USDA
    Economic Research Report Number 173, September 2014,
    www.ers.usda.gov, 41 (www.ers.usda.gov/publications/err-
    economic-research-report/err173.aspx).

5   Ibid.

6   DeNavas-Walt, 13.

7   Nicholas Kristof, "An Idiot's Guide to Inequality," *New York Times*, July 24, 2014.

8   Mark Mather, "U.S. Children in Single-Mother Families," *Population Reference Bureau*, May 2010, www.prb.org.

9   "Poverty and Its Measurement," *Instituto Nacional de Estadistica*, 2009, 2-3, www.ine.es/en/daco/daco42/sociales/pobreza_en.pdf.

10 Dr. David Gordon, University of Bristol, "Indicators of Poverty & Hunger", December 12-14, 2005, 4 http://www.un.org/esa/socdev/unyin/documents/ydiDavidGordon_poverty.pdf.

11 http://siteresources.worldbank.org/INTPOVERTY/Resources/335642-1124115102975/1555199-1124115187705/ch2.pdf.

12 "The State of the World's Children," *UNICEF*, 2010, 18-19, www.unicef.org/sowc.

13 Gerhard Peters and John T. Woolley, "Special Message to the Congress," *The American Presidency Project*, March 16, 1964, www.presidency.ucsb.ed/ws/?pid=26109.

14 Drew Desilver, "Who's poor in America? 50 years into the 'War on Poverty,' a data portrait" Pew Research Center, January 13, 2014 (http://pewrsr.ch/1cWtBk1).

15 Suzanne Macartney, "Child Poverty in the United States 2009 and 2010: Selected Race Groups and Hispanic Origin," *American Community Survey Briefs*, November 2011, www.census.gov/prod/2013/pubs/acsbr11-17.pdf.

16 Alemayehu Bishaw and Kayla Fontenot, "Poverty: 2012 and 2013, American Community Survey Briefs," September 2014,

1 (http://www.census.gov/content/dam/Census/library/publications/2014/acs/acsbr13-01.pdf).

17 USDA statistics, 2012. http://ers.usda.gov/data-products/county-level-data-sets/poverty.aspx.

18 Department of Health and Human Services (DHHS), Healthy People 2020. http://www.healthypeople.gov/2020/data-search.

19 "Medical Expenditure Panel Survey (MEPS)," *Agency for Health Research and Quality (AHRQ)*, www.meps.ahrq.gov/mepsweb/.

20 David Cecere, Cambridge Health Alliance, *Harvard Gazette*, September 17, 2009, http://news.harvard.edu/gazette/story/2009/09/new-study-finds-45000-deaths-annually-linked-to-lack-of-health-coverage/.

21 Steven H. Woolf and Laudan Aron, Editors, "U.S. Health in International Perspective Shorter Lives, Poorer Health," National Research Council and Institute of Medicine, The National Academies Press. Copyright 2013. http://obssr.od.nih.gov/pdf/IOM%20Report.pdf.

22 Howard Steven Friedman, "America's Poverty-Education Link," *The Huffington Post*, October 29, 2012, www.huffingtonpost.com.

23 Myles Munroe, *A Kingdom Book* (Shippensburg, PA Destiny Image Publishers, 2008), 68-69.

24 Ron Nixon, "Farm Bill Compromise Will Change Programs and Reduce Spending" *The New York Times*, January 27, 2014, http://www.nytimes.com/2014/01/28/us/politics/farm-bill-compromise-will-reduce-spending-and-change-programs.html.

25 "Homeless Youth" National Coalition for the Homeless, factsheet published June 2008. http://nationalhomeless.org/factsheets/youth.html.

26 Dr. Wayne W. Dyer, *The Shift,* directed by Michael Goorjian, executive producer Reid Tracy. Hay House DVD.

27 "HIV in the United States: At A Glance," Centers for Disease Control and Prevention, November 2014, http://www.cdc.gov/hiv/pdf/statistics_basics_ataglance_factsheet.pdf

28 David D. Burstein, *Fast Future* (Boston, Beacon Press, 2013), xvi.

29 "Millennials: A Portrait of Generation Next," *Pew Research Center*, Feb. 24, 2010, www.pewresearch.org/millenials. http://www.pewsocialtrends.org/files/2010/10/millennials-confident-connected-open-to-change.pdf.

30 World Health Organization "Child marriages: 39,000 every day", March 7, 2013, http://www.who.int/mediacentre/news/releases/2013/child_marriage_20130307/en/.

31 Marvin J. Cetron and Owen Davies, "52 Trends Shaping Tomorrow's World," *The Futurist,* May/June, 2010, 13.

32 Jim Collins, *Good to Great* (New York, Harper Collins, 2001) 20-22.

33 Collins, *Good to Great*, 20-22.

34 Deepak Chopra, *The Soul of Leadership* (New York: Harmony Books, 2010), 89.

35 Small Business Administration SBA, Office of Advocacy, March 2014.

36 William Eggers and Paul Macmillan, *The Solution Revolution* (Boston: Harvard Business Review Press, 2013), 18-19.

37 NikeInc. FY12/13 Sustainable Business Performance Summary. http://www.nikeresponsibility.com/report/uploads/files/FY12-13_NIKE_Inc_CR_Report.pdf 32, 55.

38 Coca-Cola Corporate Social Responsibility Report, 2011.

39 Coca-Cola Sustainability Report/Water Stewardship, 2011/2012.

40 Eggers and Macmillan, *The Solution Revolution*, (Boston, Harvard Business Review Press, 2013). 37

41 www.abillionpluschange.org

42 Ron Brookmeyer, Sarah Gray, and Claudia Kawas, "Projections of Alzheimer's Disease in the United States and the impact of delaying disease onset," *American Journal of Public Health*, September 1998: 1337-1342. http://www.ncbi.nlm.nih.gov/pmc/articles/instance/1509089/.

43 Joel Osteen, *Your Best Life Now* (Warner Faith, New York, 2004), 208.

44 Stephen Covey, *The 8th Habit: From Effectiveness to Greatness* (New York: Simon & Schuster, 2004), 53.

45 Dr. Wayne W. Dyer, *Change Your Thoughts* (New York: Hay House USA, 2007), 119.

46 Chopra, *The Soul of Leadership,* 135.

47 Dyer, *The Power of Intention* (New York: Hay House 2008), 4.

48 2001 Census and The World Factbook, CIA, https://www.cia.gov/library/publications/the-world-factbook/geos/print/country/countrypdf_up.pdf.

49 Iryna Prymachyk, "Reports of racist attacks down, but problem persists," *Kyiv Post*, April 21, 2010.

50 Dr. Wayne W. Dyer, *Change Your Thoughts*, 259.

51 Lucinda Vardey, *Mother Teresa, A Simple Path* (New York: Ballantine Books, 1995), 185.

About the Author

Juanita Farrow, an authority on entrepreneurship, business, and consulting for more than twenty years, is also a former adjunct professor, hospital administrator and the founder and president of a consulting company specializing in government contracts and grants. In recent years, she was appointed to serve on Virginia's Veterans Services Foundation board, and is now an inspirational speaker and business and global healthcare consultant.

Printed in the USA
CPSIA information can be obtained
at www.ICGtesting.com
JSHW082348140824
68134JS00020B/1952